Wicca for Beginners

A Guide to Witchcraft, Rituals, Spells, Moon Magic and Wiccan Beliefs

Kevin Patterson

The information stated herein is provided for educational purposes exclusively. The presentation of the data is without contractual agreement or any kind of warranty assurance.

All trademarks inside this book are for clarifying purposes only and are possessed by the owners themselves, not allied with this document.

Disclaimer

All erudition supplied in this book is specified for educational and academic purposes only. The author is not in any way to be responsible for any outcomes that emerge from using this book. Constructive efforts have been made to render information that is both precise and effective. Still, the author is not to be held answerable for the accuracy or use/misuse of this information.

Foreword

I will like to thank you for taking the very first step of trusting me and deciding to purchase/read this life-transforming book. Thanks for investing your time and resources on this product.

I can assure you of precise outcomes if you will diligently follow the specific blueprint I lay bare in the information handbook you are currently checking out. It has transformed lives, and I firmly believe it will equally change your own life too.

All the information I provided in this Do It Yourself piece is easy to absorb and practice.

Table of Contents

INTRODUCTION

This book is geared toward the solitary practitioner who wishes to discover ways to practice Wicca but is not sure of how to start. The book does not support or recommend any particular Wiccan tradition or ideology; instead, it focuses on the beliefs most Wiccans have in common. Reading this book is an excellent way to begin for those curious about Wicca.

Take time to learn the subtle nuances upon which the craft is based. By doing this, you will gain essential understanding, and you require to genuinely make the most of all the art needs to provide. Wicca is more than a once-in-a-week journey to the church; it is a lifestyle.

If you're reading this book, you probably currently understand Witches and Wiccans are real people, living in the contemporary world-- not the mean, green-faced, frightening old hags seen in popular movies and Halloween outfits.

They are not malicious, and they don't attempt to manipulate anybody through sneaky means.

Although lots of Wiccans and Witches might be deceptive about their work and faith, there is absolutely nothing ominous about what they do. These stereotypes arise from misunderstandings about pagan beliefs discovered throughout Europe before the rise of Christianity.

This has prevented lots of people from knowing anything about the luxurious appeal of the customs for those following the spiritual lifestyle. Happily, you will soon know more about the realities, instead of the misconceptions about Wicca.

Interest in Wicca has increased significantly over the years. This is at least in part, thanks to the internet. Just about twenty years back, those people curious about this subject might have had limited access to important information, especially those without an excellent New Age or Occult book shop anywhere in the area. The internet has made it easy for information to get to whoever seeks it. Not every website is of equivalent quality, of course, and people are mostly advised to overlook anything that does not "feel" right for them. This is true for print sources, too.

Wiccan authors can sometimes be argumentative-- as individuals enthusiastic about any religious beliefs can be-- and you might discover that some sources resonate with you more than others.

This book is meant as a quick introduction to the subject, covering one of the most fundamental concerns that people curious about Wicca tend to have.

We will be checking out the faith of Wicca, the history of its modern-day origins, and the fundamental belief systems that its different traditions commonly hold. Then, we will carry on to magic, as we look at Wiccan practices, including the relationship between witchcraft and magic, and covering a few of the necessary tools and methods involved.

CHAPTER ONE

Understanding Wicca

The Meaning of Wicca

Wicca is categorized as a nature-based faith incorporating a wide array of customs, practices, and beliefs influenced by several sources-- Wiccans typically refer to these sources as "the Old Religion."

There are many types of customs under the umbrella of Wicca, generally with overlapping aspects such as pantheism, polytheism, an emphasis on routine, and deep respect for all living things.

Wicca has been mostly referred to as a shamanic religion. "Shamanism" is a term initially used to refer to ancient religious beliefs found in areas of Asia. Still, it has since been used in describing numerous indigenous customs throughout the world whose origins predate recorded history. Shamanism is mostly called the world's first religion, although it would not have appeared like the significant religions these days with their consistent beliefs and constant practices that span continents.

Features of shamanic traditions include an animistic world view, using altered states of consciousness to interact with the spirit world, and using the knowledge found there for healing and the basic well-being of the community. Shamans were the very first "medication individuals" and were revered in their societies. Like shamans, Wiccans look for a connection with the hidden spirits of nature and work with natural representatives such as stones and herbs for protection and healing.

Wicca is also thought about to be a Pagan faith. Like "shamanism," "paganism" is also an umbrella term. It has been specified in the broadest sense as any religion that is not Christianity, Judaism, or Islam. Still, it's more accurate to say that Paganism involves nature-based belief systems that mostly (however not always) include several deities.

The word "pagan" originates from the Latin, where it implies "country individual," and didn't have any religious association. Later, the name took on an unfavorable connotation when Christianity attempted to stamp out the old beliefs and practices of the country occupants in Europe and other places it looked for to control.

As a nature-based collection of practices and beliefs, Wicca is a kind of paganism, but there are lots of other contemporary Pagan traditions besides Wicca. This difference is intended more at modern-day (or "Neopagan") spiritual movements than the general sense of the word as a category of "faith." "The Old Religion" isn't found in a specific text or location or culture, but is a sort of catch-all name for the many hairs of older spiritual and cultural beliefs that notify today's practices.

While it claims spiritual roots in older pagan and shamanic belief systems, Wicca itself is a contemporary religious belief, of relatively recent origins, and the word "Wicca" as an official name for the faith came about several years after its preliminary starting. Considering that there is no consensus on any particular text, practice, or specific belief, there is a great deal of leeway in regards to who may "claim" to be Wiccan. However, many practices overlap among different customs, groups, and people.

Among the elements of Wicca that distinguish it from other more commonly acknowledged religious beliefs is its emphasis on the feminine, as signified by nature, the Earth, the Moon, and feminine divine beings (or goddesses). The masculine is also represented through deity and is primarily associated with the

Sun, but there is none of the patriarchy typically discovered in other Western faiths.

Belief systems and practices identifying as Wiccan can be highly formalized and consist of hierarchical structures within practicing groups, but can also be very personalized and "free-form."

Wicca's modern history is complete of unusual and intriguing characters whose different contributions to the practice are a subject of much research study and argument by today's historians of the movement. Before diving into the critical points of Wicca's origins, let's look at some of the terms often associated with the name "Wicca.".

Historical Facts About Wicca.

To comprehend modern Wicca, its wisdom and practices, what you'll be doing, and why it's crucial to understand where it comes from. There's been no little effort and debate in understanding Wicca's origins and development. All faiths have myths about their starts, but when it comes to Wicca, the reality is more remarkable than the misconception. There are important reasons that Wicca is called the Craft of the Wise.

Roots

The word itself is a great place to start. Wicca arrived in Britain with the Anglo- Saxons in the mid-5th century. Its roots go back some 5,500 years to the most widely spoken language in the world, called Proto-Indo-European. There are also roots to prophecy, or talking to divinity.

How did Wicca get connected to Witch? Simple: the pronunciation of Wicca is witch-a, and in the 16th century, the Modern English spelling ended up being Witch. The origin of both words provides a different picture from the negative stereotype of the evil, Satan-worshipping hag, and reminds us that there were Indigenous traditions in England, and, throughout Europe and the Fertile Crescent (the Middle East), long before the arrival of Christianity and the vicious stereotype.

Wicca and Shamanism

Wicca is rooted in shamanism, humankind's earliest spirituality. Some call it the Old Religion. Today shamanism is still practiced throughout the world by around 370 million Indigenous individuals, despite centuries of harsh colonial domination.

A modern-day form of core shamanism, made up of essential practices common to lots of shamanic traditions but without specific cultural overlays, is being significantly practiced by the modern descendants of immigrants from Europe, Russia, Africa, and in other places who are also uncovering their Indigenous ancestral traditions.

Shamans are masters of balancing, harmonizing, and uniting inner and outer, the visible and invisible, the world, and the spirit. Across the world, shamans use comparable strategies to open themselves to the Sacred and to live in consistency with nature. They shift and begin their awareness with ecstatic practices like drumming, chanting, dancing, journeying, praying, vision-seeking, communion with sacred plants, working with natural energies and aspects, routine and ceremony.

Not everyone ends up being a shaman, but anyone can practice shamanism. Not everybody ends up being a Priest/ess, but anyone can practice Wicca. For hundreds of years, practicing

Wicca, practicing Witchcraft, or even being accused of being a Wiccan could get you eliminated.

Rebirth

In the early 1930s, an impressive group of English critics went looking for the religious beliefs of their ancestors. Why that moment? Perhaps it was a response to100 years of the Industrial Revolution, with its damage to land and people, and the penalizing effects of World War I and the Great Depression.

Inspiration may also have come from the counterculture of Romantics, Spiritualists, Suffragists, Theosophists and the mystical, incredible motion made famous by the Hermetic Order of the Golden Dawn-- a metaphysical society with such distinguished members as Lady Gregory and the poet W.B. Yeats-- all trying to find a different type of divinity that consisted of the Feminine Principle.

These brave souls lived in the middle of enormous stone circles, gigantic mounds and chalk giants sculpted into hillsides stories of fairies and myths of Avalon, the Green Knight and Sir Gawain, seasonal stag-antlered dances and the faces of Green Men carved in churches, Goddesses called Bride, Brigid and Brigantia, from whom some say the name Britain came, and Gods of the forest such as Cernunnos and Herne. There was seasonal rejoicing remembered in regional folk traditions and protected within the Christian calendar, and old Gods and Goddesses very finely disguised as saints. Everything was amber in which proof of an earlier life resided.

There was also the advanced theory of a fantastic Egyptologist and Suffragist, Dr. Margaret Murray, the 'grandmother of Wicca.' Murray's book, The Witch-Cult in Western Europe, released by Oxford University Press in1921, argued that Witchcraft had been a pan-European religious practice with beliefs, rituals, and systems as developed as that of any.

Whatever the inspiration, it's challenging to recover a religion from shattered shards and a bad reputation. Three covens, or groups, appeared in England in Hampshire's New Forest and Norfolk and Cheshire. The covens were discreet and hidden, but in 1951, the Witchcraft Law of 1735 was rescinded, and Witchcraft burst into the general public's awareness in the individual of Gerald Gardner, a retired British civil servant.

Gardner wrote many of the very first books on Witchcraft by a practitioner and spoke publicly and to journalists-- no little accomplishment given the lingering stereotypes. And he dealt with a few of the most crucial females in Wicca, like Doreen Valiente, the coven's High Priestess. Valiente wrote the famous Goddess invocation The Charge of the Goddess, and she and Gardner expanded the rites and practices that formed the structure of the Gardnerian custom.

Gardner declared that he practiced the faith Murray had described, calling it Wicca, and her theory ended up being Wicca's well-accepted 'misconception of origin.' Years later, after thorough scrutiny, practitioners and historians concluded that the Gardnerian custom was not an unbroken, hereditary, pan-European tradition matching Murray's theory.

Today, many people still register for Murray's theory as a literal fact. Always, other Wiccans appreciate her recognition of stereotypical truths that continue to resonate-- a Great Mother Goddess, a Horned God of forest and field, a little community arranged into groups (covens) with skilled Priestesses and Priests, using thrilling practices, the celebration of seasonal, lunar rites and holy days, initiation rites and the keeping of a book of wisdom called the Book of Shadows.

Wicca settled and started to grow beyond the British Isles with the rediscovery of other forgotten Euro-Indigenous traditions and pantheons of divine beings from faiths that existed before the Abrahamic religious beliefs (Judaism, Christianity, and Islam), particularly Goddesses, which were incorporated into Wiccan practice and cosmology. Ladies found a spiritual home that honored them as religious leaders; publishing and the internet also connected people and offered access. Leaders who were unafraid of persecution emerged into the public eye to challenge stereotypes, and the motion grew and generated a more comprehensive revival of Modern and euro-indigenous pagan traditions.

Today, there are lots of variations and varied family trees and customs in Wicca, each with its organizational structure. Many have included religious organizations, churches, or temples, and while the law and academics now recognize Wicca as a spiritual practice, many practitioners choose the term spirituality. In formal studies, the number of followers of Wicca varies from a couple of hundred thousand to several million worldwide.

Wiccans are lawyers, physicians, rock stars, truck motorists, dog fitness instructors, and Unitarian ministers and as most likely to be your neighbor next door as your dental expert. Wiccans are, literally, everywhere.

Wicca's legitimacy does not need to be obtained from its past, but from the profound, transformative spiritual experiences, worths and insights it provides professionals every day. In this sense, Wicca is a brand-new mental motion, and its (re)birth is among the rarest and significant occasions in human history.

The origin of Wicca traces back to a British occultist named Gerald Gardner in the early 1940s. Gardner's frustration with both Ceremonial Magic, the only "occult" option and Christianity, prompted him to create something that appears to be different in some ways.

Gerald Gardner's religious practice was based on pre-existing spiritual principles, which he integrated in a new way to form a brand-new system. His mixing of ceremonial magic with hereditary Witchcraft and Masonic ritual was nothing less than genius. And, with the assistance of individuals like Doreen Valiente, Dion Fortune, Ross Nichols, and other notable scholars, he could develop a vibrant and new religion.

Witchcraft, or Wicca, as we understand it today, is not the sole survivor of antiquity, nor is it a modern creation. Instead, it is a mix of many various spiritual persuasions. Even though Pagan rites, Shamanic customs, and Goddess worship predate Christianity, there is still no reputable proof of a recognized Wiccan religion before the year 1951.

Gerald Gardner broke the vow of secrecy after the final repeal of the English Witchcraft Act in1951, by accepting the New Forest Coven.

Today, many Wiccan organizations in the United States and Europe support Gerald Gardner's ideas.

The Known History

The modern origins of Wicca can be traced back to the British Occult motion in the late 19th century. A couple of crucial figures credited with advancing and establishing Wicca as a faith are Gerald Gardner, Cecil Williamson, Patricia Crowther, and Lois Bourne. Gardner (1884-1964) is widely credited as being the creator of Wicca. However, he and his fellow witches didn't use the term "Wicca" as a recognizing term, but instead called their practice "Witchcraft," (in some cases reduced to "the Craft") or "the Old Religion." Gardner did describe the members of his custom as "The Wicca," but "Wicca" as a name for the religion was not used frequently up until the 1960s as it affected the U.S. and Australia.

Gardner had ended up being interested in a theory advanced in the early 1920s by anthropologist Margaret Murray (1863-1963), which held that a pagan religious belief with a family tree going back to ancient times had existed in secret throughout the rise and supremacy of Christianity in Western Europe. Murray called this faith a "witch cult" and asserted that its professionals were arranged into 13-member groups or covens, and worshipped a male "horned" god.

In the early 1940s, Gardner's exploration of occult and mystical experiences influenced him to develop a brand-new incarnation of the witch-cult, and he formed the Bricket Wood coven. Blending concepts from Murray with other sources such as Freemasonry, ceremonial magic, and the work of other Occult authors, Gardner's custom broadened the divine being praise to include a female goddess component along with the male god.

In 1947, Gardner met and befriended Aleister Crowley (1875-1947), a well-known occultist and writer. They had checked out and taken part in a variety of spiritual and esoteric customs from worldwide, consisting of Buddhism, Jewish mysticism, Hinduism, the Tarot, astrology, and more. Crowley's writings had a considerable impact on Gardner, who included some of the rituals devised by Crowley in his work. It was Crowley who coined the spelling of "magick" with a "k" to distinguish his type of magic from other "ritualistic magic"-- and even stage magic-- practices of the time.

Crowley is a complex figure for lots of Wiccans today. Some of the practices he took part in were considered to be scandalous, and his role in the history of the religious beliefs helped perpetuate an incorrect association between Wicca/Witchcraft and Satanism.

It must be remembered that "Satanism" belongs to the Christian world view and not a pagan idea, which Wicca does not, and never did, integrate, endorse, or practice "Satanism" or the worship of anything "evil.".

Crowley had a reputation for being misogynist and racist, which are mindsets incompatible with the Wiccan way of life. At any rate, the custom now referred to as Gardnerian Wicca began to grow as Gardner brought other interested Occultists into his coven, consisting of several women, among whom was Doreen Valiente (1922-1999). Valiente ended up being the High Priestess of Bricket Wood in the early 1950s and revised much of the initial material the coven had been using, in part because she felt it had too much of Crowley's influence. Ultimately, Valiente parted methods with Gardner over what she perceived to be his careless attempts to make modern Witchcraft known to the masses, and his decision to restrict the power of ladies in the coven in response to their criticisms.

Valiente formed her coven in 1957 and went on to study Witchcraft with other leading figures in the movement, eventually composing several prominent books that assisted introduce the evolution of Witchcraft from a secret society phenomenon to a widespread, highly customized practice. Other notable figures in the growth of the Craft were Alex Sanders (1926-1988), who established the Alexandrian tradition of Wicca, and Raymond Buckland, who formed the Seax-Wicca custom in the early 1970s. Born in 1934, Buckland is credited with bringing Gardnerian Wicca to the United States and has written dozens of books on Witchcraft and other esoteric subjects.

It was during the 2nd half of the 20th century that what is jointly called Wicca spread from England to the rest of the United Kingdom and the United States and Australia, branching off into numerous different traditions. While those who follow the Gardnerian customs and its direct offshoots commonly draw a difference between Wicca and other, non-Wiccan witchcraft, many individuals identify as Wiccans no matter the origins of their particular practice. These consist of individuals following Dianic, Celtic, and Georgian customs, in addition to "diverse" methods adapted from a variety of traditions.

The Unknown History

Regardless of the claims of Margaret Murray, Gardner, and others to have discovered and restored an authentic ancient tradition, scholastic historians never might see much undeniable evidence to support the "witch-cult" theory. And within the motion, leaders' claims of hypnotic trance states, being "descendants" of ancient Witch lineages or "reincarnations" of Witches from past centuries, were, in some cases, questioned, even by other Witches.

Stress and anxiety over the viewed degree of validity and credibility of Wicca may have caused some Witches to take strong positions in favor of one tradition over others, one belief over another, and to argue nonstop about it. It's also possible that these concerns of authenticity led some Witches to draw more greatly from what is understood about traditions from other cultures and other mystical practices than from the particular product that was expected to link the contemporary religion straight to its ancient past.

Yet, with all that is unidentified about the past individuals and cultures that Wicca draws motivation from, what is understood is that there was some energetic phenomenon that was magical enough to keep a hold on humanity, even though the rise of Christianity and its eventual domination of the parts of the world most regularly associated with the "ancient religion." European folk magic customs, a lot of which are included in Wiccan magic, were perhaps descended from this very same source. And we likewise understand that pagans and shamans of cultures around the world looked for to engage with the hidden world in comparable ways, through music, dance, and modified states of consciousness.

It may be enough to say that what the initial creators of modern-day Wicca did was develop new kinds through which individuals could tap into the magical, bridging the space in between the modern and ancient worlds with new expressions of a magical energy that has continuously existed. There may be a dizzying range of analyses of these brand-new forms, but there suffice commonness amongst them, and adequate people participating, to make it clear the "Old Religion" is back, and here to stay.

CHAPTER TWO

Forms of Wicca

Gardnerian Wicca

Gerald Gardner set a precedent for the contemporary Wiccan motion. At some point during the late 1930s, Gardner was introduced to a genetic Witch called Old Dorothy Clutterbuck, who started him into a group called the New Forest Coven. Before this, Gardner had been added to the Masons, Oriental mysticism, and the Golden Dawn system of ritualistic magic.

Gardner's new faith did not blossom overnight. It took years to best, with the input of other Witches and occultists.

The religion that Gardner developed, Gardnerian Wicca, worries the praise of the horned God and the Goddess. A High Priestess usually heads covens, and they have three levels of initiation, paralleling those of the Masons. Religious celebrations happen at the eight seasonal shifts, and complete moons are considered to be a time of terrific power and potential.

A lot of Gardnerian groups work skyclad (naked), and polarity (the balance between the manly and feminine) is emphasized. Covens tend to have equivalent numbers of male and female initiates, and couples are motivated to join.

Alexandrian Wicca

Alexandrian Wicca, a spin-off of Gardnerian Wicca, was founded in the early 1960s by Alex Sanders and his better half, Maxine. He proclaimed himself "King of the Witches"; he declared to have been initiated at age Seven by his grandma.

Alexandrian Wiccans use Kabbalah, the excellent system of the ancient Enochian and Hebrews, the established magical language for angels, which has its alphabet and grammar. Covens often meet once a week.

Dianic Wicca

There are two distinct categories of Dianic Wicca. The first category is Old Dianic, formed in the early 1960s by Morgan McFarland and Mark Roberts. This original branch of Dianic Wicca places primary significance upon the Goddess, but still acknowledges and honors the Horned God as her accompaniment.

The 2nd branch of Dianic Witchcraft is feminist in orientation. Only females are permitted, and just the Goddess is worshiped. Frequently covens have lesbian participants just. The majority of groups are loosely structured, routines are often experimental and spontaneous, and meaning will differ from one group to another. The focus is mostly on the female aspect, and there is usually a political list attached to the group.

Diverse Wicca

This branch of Wicca covers individuals and groups who do not follow any single tradition, but who instead incorporate the elements of many different cultures into their practices. They deal with different divine beings from various pantheons, rather than focusing on one specific god and goddess. Diverse Wiccans mix and match events, myths, and symbols according to choice and experience.

Hereditary/Traditional Wicca.

The witchcraft practiced within a family that claims a lineage predating the Gardnerian revival is regarded as traditional or genetic.

Typically, the Hereditary Witch originates from a family that practiced folk magic and organic medication. When it comes to a true Hereditary Witch, there will be proof of the direct line of descent from ancestors who were Witches.

Hereditary/Traditional Witches have a slightly different approach to doing things than the post-Gardnerian Wiccans do. Generally, the majority do not use the basic set of excellent tools, but depend on everyday items to work as symbols of their craft. The importance is put on nature divine beings, fertility, appeals, amulets, and organic potions. Complete moons are usually used for divination, and the working of magic, and seasonal celebrations concentrate on the prosperity and protection of the family.

CHAPTER THREE

WhatDoWiccansBelieve?

Is Wicca a religion?

Wicca is far less organized and noticeable than other faiths such as Judaism, Christianity, or Islam, Wicca has actually been acknowledged as being entitled to the same spiritual defenses by courts in the United States. It is even considered in the chaplain's handbook of the U.S. Army. In the UK, Wiccan priestesses and priests are authorized to function as jail chaplains, but Wicca is not formally acknowledged as a religion.

Wicca is often referred to by those outside the practice as a "cult," possibly because it's called one in the Oxford English Dictionary. This word is also challenging. "Cult" has several neutral significances, though regrettably for Wiccans, it's typically associated with negative images and groups with charismatic leaders like the followers of Jim Jones. Regardless, "cult" is not generally used by Wiccans to describe Wicca.

Many authors on the subject describe Wicca as a religious belief, particularly those who identify as Wiccans. Others who use the terms "Wicca" or "Wiccan" to explain their beliefs and practices do not necessarily regard Wicca as a faith that they follow or "belong to." This may be because Wicca has no central text, prophet, or another source of authority like the dominant Western religions, and its structures and kinds of worship differ exceptionally commonly. It might also be because the word "religion" has associations that some Wiccans are not usually comfortable with.

For numerous reasons, the number of people identifying as Wiccans in predominately English-speaking countries is more difficult to accurately approximate than it is for more dominant religious beliefs. Many people choose not to disclose their religion in a culture where it is not respected and is frequently sufficient, even hostilely opposed. Others who may freely identify as Wiccans are innumerable, as there are no official holy places for them to be members of.

Some scholars evaluating random phone surveys over the past few decades have estimated that close to one million people around the world consider themselves Wiccans, with the majority found in the U.S. and the U.K. Whatever the actual count might be, it's clear that the numbers are increasing progressively in the 21st century, as more knowledge about the religious beliefs become offered and widely shared.

What's the distinction between a witch and a Wiccan?

Depending upon who you ask, there's a significant distinction, or there's not much (if any) difference.

In regards to language, the words "witch" and "Wicca" are somehow related, as "Wicca" was the Old English word that later ended up being "witch." Nevertheless, among Wiccans, the relationship between the two concepts is less black-and-white-- some Witches determine as Wiccans.

Witches who don't, and Witches who don't have a preference. Some Wiccans do not determine as Witches.

The different uses of these words can be seen throughout contemporary composing about Wicca and Witchcraft. In addition to the name of the religion, some authors use "Wicca" as a particular word in place of "Witch," but most use "Wicca" as a plural term, implying that some (or all) Wiccans can be jointly called "the Wicca.".

While the words "Wicca" and "Wiccan" tend to be capitalized-- specifically about the faith and its members-- however there appear to be no hard and fast guidelines relating to whether to capitalize the words "Witch" and "Witchcraft" or leave them in lower case.

Some fans of Wiccan customs which do not adopt the name "Wicca" as a personal identifier feel no need to recognize with a capital "W" for "Witch" or "Witchcraft." Others think that capitalization of these terms is essential in differentiating Wicca as an official religious beliefs and developing a cultural regard for it. In the spirit of respect for those who feel profoundly about acknowledging Wicca as a religion, this book capitalizes all four terms.

What's the difference between Wicca and Witchcraft?

Wiccans who don't identify as Witches do not use the term "Witchcraft" in association with their practice of Wicca-- they don't use magic, and they distinguish between Wicca as a spiritual practice and specific relationship with the divine, and witchcraft as a practice that is not always spiritual.

Many Wiccans do blend magic into their practice to varying degrees, and might usee "magic" as an interchangeable term with.

" Witchcraft" (frequently reduced to "the Craft") in association with Wicca.

In reality, some Witches who practice Witchcraft do not identify as Wiccan at all.

What does Wicca pertain to magic?

Once again, it depends upon who you ask, and for Wiccans who do not practice magic of any kind, the response is most likely "nothing." Many Wiccans do consist of magic in their practice, to the point that the two are combined in many Wiccan books and resources-- including this particular book!

Many Witches will refer to their practice of magic as Witchcraft, but might use either term. And of course, the word "magic" is also a bit tricky, as it has its own set of meanings.

" Ceremonial magic" is older than Wicca and was an initial impact for what would eventually end up being Wicca. However, it's, in fact, a practice in its own right-- to put it simply, not part of the religious beliefs. This ritualistic magic has numerous differences from the magic practiced by Witches. Ceremonial magic was derived from occult customs through secret societies like the Freemasons and the Hermetic Order of the Golden Dawn, and is typically quite elaborately ritualized. The term "high magic" is, in some cases, used to differentiate it from Witchcraft, which is called "folk magic" or perhaps "low magic" by numerous of its practitioners. Some who practice ceremonial magic may determine as Pagans but are not Wiccans or Witches. Some merely discover as magicians.

What some call "useful magic" is a sort of ceremonial magic focused on attaining common life improvements, such as healing physical or emotional ills, drawing in love, and improving one's financial resources. Some Wiccans see this form of magic as non-spiritual and distinct from Wicca, but others mix the two by performing magic in positioning with their deities and for the good of all, instead of just for their own personal gain.

Wiccans Believe Everything Is Connected

Many people discover Wicca in pieces and bits. Maybe Wiccan routine empowers them. Or the Wiccan respect the rhythms and cycles of nature that pleases them. Or magic interests them. To fully discover and comprehend the significance in Wicca, a person needs to grasp the vast image of the Wiccan worldview.

A couple of core concepts underlie all of Wicca, and if you understand these standard principles about the divine and the entire world, then Wiccan beliefs and practices make sense. This chapter supplies the background to comprehend Wicca as a full-fledged spirituality and a specific method of experiencing and translating the world.

Swimming in a Divine Sea of Energy

You will discover one principle that is essential to the Wiccan belief, which "is: Everything is linked."

Everything that exists becomes part of an unbroken circle of vibrating energy. You might discover it uses to picture truth as a web of energy. Some individuals refer to this idea as the web of life or nature's web. Most Wiccans think that Deity is imminent (is right here, today, and all-present in the world) and also appears in the environment (is apparent and quickly viewed).

The majority believe that whatever exists streams from the Deity. The Divine is regarded as the source of all life. Some Wiccans even think that the entire universes are the living body of Deity.

The belief in Deity gives faith. Nobody can prove that the universes have a Divine source; however, but honestly, there is one big, connected, boundless network.

Finding Kinship right in the Cosmos

The Wiccan perception of an interconnected world isn't merely a magical, spiritual concept. Modern science, particularly cutting-edge ideas in quantum physics, supports the concepts of life's affiliation and interdependence. Below are some of the leading theories that mix thoroughly with Wiccan belief.

Going quantum: Matter versus energy

Individuals see the real world as a bunch of steady and independent objects. However, that's not precisely the reality. Modern science exposes that matter and energy are not different.

Energy streams in waves that form patterns. What you view as a different thing (a pet dog, a bird, or a tree) is just a pocket of truth where the energy is more dense, according to quantum physics

Quantum physics.

Physical matter is made up of particles and atoms, which are comprised of smaller components, referred to as subatomic particles. A subatomic particle is not precisely a little dot of matter that scientists can hold still and analyze; it's better described as a bit of dancing point of energy. These particles can't be comprehended as different units. Scientists can describe subatomic particles just by discussing how they show one another. The best way to meaningfully describe these particles is to discuss the way that they adjoin.

String theory.

A subatomic particle is not pointlike; however, it is made of a small loop. Like an incredibly- thin elastic band, each particle contains a vibrating, dancing string. Like a guitar string, each low string can vibrate. Every line equals; the only distinction is how it vibrates. Each series has various vibration like each guitar string develops distinct musical notes. The motions of the series-- the "note" it produces-- identify the kind of particle it will be. These itty-bitty vibrating strings comprise everything in the universe-- all physical matter and all forces (such as gravity). These strings vibrate throughout space-time.

We reside in space-time. Space-time consists of three dimensions of area (width, depth, and length) and the proportion of the time. All objects and all events exist in these four measurements. Well, that's what scientists utilized to believe. According to the string theory, space-time can have up to nine measurements of space, plus the analysis of time.

Wicca meets string theory.

String theory unites matter and energy and validates the Wiccan view that the universe from the smallest particles to the most significant planetary systems operates by the same principles and is made from the same stuff. At all levels, life is adjoined.

They are spreading out the turmoil.

String theory indicates the interconnection of life at all levels, big and small. Chaos theory deals just with the vast and super-complicated.

Chaos theory

Chaos theory recommends that the weather and other massive, complicated systems in nature have an underlying order, but they are virtually unforeseeable and chaotic. The issue with predicting the weather and the habits of other big systems is that life is very conscious of altering conditions. Minimal modifications can have significant impacts. Any small inaccuracy in assessing the preliminary conditions results in growing errors in the calculations.

The significant lesson here is that any action, no matter how little or irrelevant, can impact everything else. Earth's ecology is a network of relationships. All the members of the Earth's environment are synergistic. The success of the entire community depends upon each living thing, while the success of each living thing depends significantly on the success of the city. This concept forms the core of Wiccan principles.

Looking at Gaia

The world is made up of specific parts, and these parts may function by themselves. The pieces are all made of the same energy and are connected to form one giant whole. For instance:

- An individual cell forms part of a person.
- Human beings belong to life on Earth.
- Earth belongs to the planetary system.

The Gaia hypothesis

Climatic chemist James Lovelock, microbiologist Lynn Margulis, and others have established a theory referred to as the Gaia hypothesis, in honor of the Greek Goddess of the Earth. This principle explains all of Planet Earth as a living system that organizes itself and keeps all its parts in balance.

Lovelock and Margulis never suggested that Earth is a sentient being (a mindful, imaginative being). However, others have expanded the theory to reach this concept.

Enfolding and unfolding

Physicist David Bohm propounded a theory of physics on the concept that truth unfolds from one original, boundless source. Numerous charge card has these pictures. Each little piece of a hologram can recreate the entire image. In other words, each part includes all the information about the full. This structure is standard in nature. A small seed contains all the info to grow a tall sunflower.

The Holographic Universe

Based upon this design, Bohm (a former coworker of Einstein) suggested that the details for the whole universe are held in each of its parts. For Bohm, the explicate order is the different parts of the world that we see. The link order enfolds all these parts into one whole. All beings, including people, are born from this source, are connected, and share consciousness.

Wicca meets the holographic universe

The relatively new design of the Holographic Universe reflects a worldview that Pagans have held given that the most ancient times: We are all part of the Divine energy; we are all linked, and our fate is inexorably linked. Nature flows from Deity, and Wiccan spirituality focuses on the event of our connection with nature and the human place in the web of life. Much of Wiccan practice is dedicated to developing a relationship with the Divine energy, in which we are permanently ingrained.

Wiccans Believe In Deity

Most, although not all, Wiccans believe in a creative being or force. However, how Wiccans perceive and experience the Divine is unique to each person. Wiccans stretch the concept of Deity to the extreme.

Two individuals may conveniently call themselves Wiccan. They might carry out the same rituals, work the same magic, and happily practice side by side, but they might have drastically various principles of who, or what, Deity is. The majority of Wiccans would instead celebrate their distinctions than become religious beliefs in which everybody must conform to the same idea or look for the same experience.

The following areas outline some manner ins which Wiccans define the Divine. It's an overall appearance in some typical manner ins which individuals think about Deity. The details may assist you to comprehend the variety of Wicca. You might not be able to pigeonhole your own experience according to these explanations. Do not attempt to intellectually choose one of these classifications and then expect your spiritual life to conform to one of these examples outrightly. Let your religious life show what is right for you, whether it shows one, a mix, or none of

the following examples.

- **Honoring The One**

Lots of Wiccans believe in a Deity who is the source of the cosmos. The Wiccan names for this Divine power consist of, but not limited to: The All, the Ultimate Sacred, The One, the Great Mystery, Creative or Supreme Being, the Source, the All-Encompassing Unity and the Life Force.

Many think that this Deity is too vast, too complicated, too incomprehensible, and also limitless (can something be too infinite?) for the human mind ever to comprehend. Although most Wiccans acknowledge this concept of Deity, they have lots of ways of defining, perceiving, or otherwise making the principle of the Divine more workable.

- **Deity as life force**

The Divine being is the ultimate support of all that exists. All of reality is a whole network of vibrating energy, which energy is the Goddess. The entire universes is the body of the Goddess (including physical and psychological strength).

The Goddess is immanent, indicating that She is right here, today and is all-present in the world.

Deity as the Supreme Goddess.

Deity is regarded as the supreme Goddess. She is considered to be the source of all life, and the vital force flows or unfolds from Her. Goddess is the only or the main Deity, and She is a supernatural, imaginative being. He is the child, consort, or symptom of the Great Goddess if there is a God. She is understood primarily in the Mother element, often called Earth Mother or Great Goddess. She also is transcendent, in the sense that She is a thinking and creative being independent of the cosmos.

This theory is in keeping with the ideas of some early Paganism.

- **Deity as the Source**

The outlook is not standard, and some Wiccans are reconciling their spiritual beliefs with the mentors of the new physics. Lots of scientists and philosophers have recommended this kind of idea. Still, scientists and paleontologist Pierre Teilhard de Chardin and physicist David Bohm are mainly accountable for the real popularity of this particular Deity theory.

This holy intelligence existed before the universes were formed, and all reality comes from it. Because all of the truth flows from the Source, everything is linked. The Source encompasses all time and space, all dimensions, and all planes of presence. All things that exist emerge from the Source, and then everything enfolds back into the Source, in a constant cycle.

Individuals continually have brand-new experiences, and they acquire knowledge and insight. All this new info becomes part of the Source Energy, and the Source expands and develops. Individuals are part of the Source, so they likewise progress and grow, reaching higher levels of awareness. People become part of that evolution and even play an essential function in advancement.

Our intelligence and insight permits us to view the Source. Our consciousness acts as the bridge between this holy intelligence and the natural world.

Through our consciousness, we take in detail from our experiences in the world and share that information with the Source; and through our awareness, we also can receive information from the Source for usage on the planet. In computer terminology, this is a feedback loop of info.

This view follows contemporary physics. The language is present; the theory isn't so different from the old Pagan idea of the primal Goddess as both life force and innovative being.

- **Honoring the Two**

Numerous Wiccans think in The One, also referred to as the ultimate Source of the cosmos, but they see it as a type of energy field having two poles. The God and the Goddess are opposite poles of the Divine, and Wiccans honor or praise both the female and male aspects of Deity. Most of the Wiccans probably hold this view or a variation of it. However, no one can state for sure.

CHAPTER FOUR

A World In Balance: Polarity And Duality

In Wicca, particularly in particular customs, polarity or duality is an essential principle. Many Wiccans honor the duality or polarity in nature and have included the idea into their spirituality.

Here's the concept: Energy flows in two opposite directions in nature. Numerous Wiccans see the Divine in the very same method; the Goddess and the God resemble two poles on the same battery. If they were genuinely separate beings, according to these Wiccans, confusion and mayhem would rule in the world.

The Goddess

The Goddess is the womanly aspect of the Divine. She is understood as the Great Goddess, Earth Mother (or Mother Earth), the Universal Mother, the Great Mother, the Lady, and lots of other names. Numerous cultures throughout time have worshipped her.

Maiden, Mother, and Crone

In lots of traditions of Wicca, the Goddess is carefully associated with the Moon. She typically is deemed having three aspects that correspond with the phases of the Moon:

The Maiden (the Waxing Moon) represents independence and youth. She is the virgin Goddess. She is typically related to a female's wild nature and is shown as a forest Goddess in the business of animals.

The Mother (the Full Moon) represents offering birth (not only to kids, but to concepts, insight, and jobs), and likewise nurturing, sensuality, sexuality, and creativity.

The Crone (the Waning Moon) represents age, maturity, knowledge, and the command for respect.

Throughout the eight main Wiccan holidays, the Goddess shifts in Her aspects from Maiden to Mother to Crone and back to Maiden. She provides birth to the Divine God kid, nurtures Him to the adult years, joins with Him and ends up being pregnant, and rebirths Him to start the seasons again and turn the wheel of the year.

The importance of the Goddess for ladies

Since it provides a powerful spiritual alternative to ladies, lots of scientists assume that the factor that Wicca is overgrowing is. Unlike most faiths, within a Wiccan circle, a woman can honor and worship the feminine Divine.

The significance of that truth can't be overestimated. In the doctrines of lots of religions, females are, at the finest, thought about inferior to men and subject to their control. At worst, women are considered as the source of sin in the world. This religious conditioning exceptionally harms the minds of ladies.

Within Wicca, women are equal; they are not "the other." Women have authority and autonomy equivalent to males. Their lives can be changed when females experience their holiness and when they have the chance to direct their spirituality.

The God

In a lot of Wiccan books and groups, God is given less page count or time than the Goddess. In American culture, the majority of people are familiar and even conditioned to see Deity as male. The Divine womanly is a harder concept for lots of people to get their minds around, so I dedicate more of this chapter to discussing the idea.

God is regarded as the male aspect of the Divine. He frequently is represented as the Sun and is sometimes related to forests and wild animals. Many cultures, throughout time, have worshipped him. In a lot of customs of Wicca, the God is considered equivalent to the Goddess. The bulk of Wiccan groups, traditions, and covens, think about males and females to be equal.

Honoring the Many

Many Wiccans honor or praise several Deities. These may be different aspects or parts of the one Divine Source, or they may be separate entities. They may be nature spirits, supernatural beings, or something else. They may or may not have human qualities. You might hear them called The Old Ones, The Mighty Ones, or The Ancient Ones.

Some Wiccans honor and praise the Goddess and the God and feel no pressure to pick a called Deity or Deities. Other Wiccans feel very highly that individuals need to select one or more called Goddesses or Gods to honor, worship, or communicate with.

All the Gods form part of The One

Many Wiccans recognize Deity as The One-- the infinite, unknowable Source of the universes. They believe that Deity is enormous and too intricate for people to comprehend, so these Wiccans may choose to define minimal aspects, types, or parts of Deity as Goddesses and gods. Simply put, the many Goddesses and Gods are various elements or components of one Great Source. Wiccans get to that Source by interacting with their Deities. Or, possibly, that one all-encompassing Source selects to take lots of different kinds to be understandable and perceivable to people.

The Gods are separate beings

The Goddesses and Gods are different, unique, and called Divinities. Numerous different Gods and Goddesses exist, and each has its personality and realm. A few of these beings may be Gods (male) or Goddesses (female), and some might consist of both sexes or be able to move sex and gender.

Honoring the Self

For some Wiccans, Deity might be the Higher Self, Deep Self, or Soul Self (an individual's spiritual essence),

Symbols, Archetypes And Realities

For some Wiccans, Deity lies just within the human mind and imagination. Deity might be a reality or insight occurring from the personal unconscious mind or the collective unconscious shared by all humans.

The unconscious mind has two parts:

The individual unconscious is the place of everything that isn't presently mindful; however, it can be, consisting of memories that you can call quickly and those that you have buried deep in your mind.

The collective unconscious holds the built up understanding and experiences of all humankind. It carries impulses, which are patterns of behavior. An inspiration tells a bird to construct a nest, and a turtle to go to water. Humans likewise have intuitive ways of acting.

The unconscious mind doesn't have the language to express these human habits and experiences. It communicates only in photos. It uses symbols. A sign is an image or item that represents something else. The cumulative unconscious uses archetypes, symbols that prevail to all humans. A model is not an image, however a tendency for human beings to represent specific concepts with a particular sign.

An individual may be an agnostic or an atheist and still practice Wicca. Wicca is a massive camping tent. Each person's understanding and experience of Deity is unique.

Also, some Christian groups today think that anybody who worships a God aside from theirs is following Satan. It's real that Wiccans don't worship the Christian God, nor do people of numerous other religions all over the world.

Wicca and Satanism were and are entirely various and different systems of beliefs, ethics, and practices.

Believing in Magic: Where Science Meets the Craft

Magic is a process of moving and directing energy to achieve a goal, so any description of magic needs to begin with some talk about power. That's what this chapter uses: a neat little description of the different sources and types of energy.

This chapter demystifies magic. Here, you can learn what magic is. It's effective. It's profoundly stunning. And it's a genuine force that numerous Wiccans use to enhance their lives and to assist others. Furthermore, magic is a method to deepen the relationship and honor with Deity and to help the Earth and her occupants.

Tapping into Different Kinds of Energy

Lots of various cultural customs divide the self into three parts. Each part represents a different kind of human energy and power. This department is accessible in modern psychology, in numerous types of Shamanism (particularly. the Hawaiian Huna tradition), in the mentors of Jewish Kabbalah, and lots of cultures of Wicca and Witchcraft (specifically in the Faery or Feri tradition).

In this chapter, I use the model of the Three Selves-- the Spirit self, the conscious mind, and the unconscious mind-- to plainly define the three types of energy and power that are important to Wiccans, especially in the working of magic.

Drawing from the Divine: Energy of the Spirit.

The energy of the Spirit-Self is called the Aumakua in Hawaiian Huna Shamanism and the Neshemah in Kabbalah. Different books on the Craft describe this energy as Deep Self (in Starhawk's novels), High Self, Divine Self,

Real Self, or Bird Spirit. Modern psychology does not have a comparable concept; however, the Spirit-Self is directly connected to the unconscious mind.

The Spirit Self is a person's innermost resource, the place that transcends discomfort and limitation. This is the part of the Self that shelters an individual's essence, the true nature. It transcends time, existing before birth and after death.

I was thinking and talking: Energy of the mindful mind.

The energy of the mindful mind is referred to as the ego in contemporary psychology, the Uhane in Hawaiian Huna Shamanism, and the Ruach in Kabbalah. In various books on the Craft, you may see it called Talking Self (in Starhawk's books), Middle Self, or Talker.

The conscious mind is the part of the brain that functions on a daily level. The mindful mind experiences the world and interacts with language (numbers and words). It is the reasonable mind that organizes and analyzes. It likewise makes ethical judgments and manages social relationships. It translates and discovers meaning for the unconscious mind's feelings, emotions, and images. The mindful mind makes it possible for a person to comprehend spiritual practice on a logical level. Nevertheless, the unconscious mind is essential, too, to link the mindful account with the Spirit-Self or Divine Self.

Going Deep: Energy Of The Unconscious Mind.

Did you understand that the human embryo briefly establishes structures that look like the gills of a fish, along with a visible tail? This short stage of social advancement drastically reflects our animal ancestry and our long evolutionary journey. In addition to the body, the mind, too, consists of an exceptional residue of the ancient past: the cumulative unconscious, a part of the unconscious mind.

The energy of the unconscious mind is called the id in modern psychology, the Unihipili in Hawaiian Huna Shamanism, and the Nephesh in Kabbalah. In different books on the Craft, you may see it called Younger Self (in Starhawk's books), Low Self, Child Self, Young Self, Child Within, Inner Child, Animal Spirit, or Fetch.

The unconscious mind has two parts: the individual unconscious and the cumulative unconscious.

- The personal unconscious.

The personal unconscious is the location of individual information that is beyond present awareness or awareness, including memories that an individual can call up quickly, and those buried deep within the mind.

- The collective unconscious.

The collective unconscious is the inherited part of the brain. It holds the accumulated understanding and experiences of all humanity (and perhaps animals). The collective unconscious mind doesn't have lots of language abilities. It experiences the world and expresses itself in images, emotions, experiences, and dreams. It uses signs. A sign is an image or item that represents something else.

The collective unconscious contains our impulses, which are patterns of habits. Instinct tells a bird to develop a nest, and a turtle to go to water. People likewise have intuitive ways of behaving. Impulses are ways of acting. The cumulative unconscious also consists of archetypes, which are methods of perceiving. A pattern is a propensity for human beings to represent specific ideas with a particular symbol. These stereotypical symbols appear in religious beliefs, dreams, myths, and fairytales throughout all human history. The Earth Mother is an excellent example of an archetype, and the Hero is another prime example.

What does all this mind-stuff have to do with Wicca? Whatever! Many of the practices of Wiccan routine-- mainly routine performed for the function of working magic are shown to trigger the unconscious mind.

Specifically, the working of magic is more productive, more efficient, and more satisfying when the unconscious mind is included. The unconscious mind is mighty, and the images, signs, emotions, and other information hidden within it are a valuable resource for bringing and comprehending the self about modification.

Wiccans use primal images, smells, textures, and sounds to arouse the unconscious mind. Candle flames, incense, stones, and drumming are some examples of traditional components of the Craft that are utilized for this function. Spells are made to rhyme to engage the unconscious in the magic. Wiccans often raise power, which means to induce a light hypnotic trance state, to activate the unconscious mind for magical work.

Engaging the unconscious mind is essential in the working of magic for the following reasons: Exciting the unconscious mind makes a person open up to experiencing Deity since the Spirit Self or Divine Self communicates straight with the unconscious mind.

The unconscious mind drives specific habits, as well as feelings. The conscious mind may rationally understand that certain practices are unsafe or disadvantageous (for example, smoking cigarettes, drinking, or extreme gaming). However, modifying habits might be strict unless the unconscious is aroused and encouraged to play a function in personal change. Magic engages the unconscious mind, and after that, the unconscious mind influences the individual to make the magic work. This is the power of the idea.

The unconscious mind can assist create the power to shape and direct energy to change the Self or alter the world. The cumulative unconscious also may offer a link to the signed up with the awareness of all human beings, to the species as a whole. Subtly shifting the energy in the collective unconscious may produce modification on the planet beyond the self.

In addition to Deity, some Wiccans might welcome the presence or help of other kinds of energy forms or beings. These might consist of:.

Forefathers: A real relative or someone else who has passed on. Some Wiccans contact ancestors for recommendations or assistance, or to deal with exceptional psychological problems. Whether and when an individual contacts ancestors depend on the person's outlook on the afterlife, reincarnation is a frequently held belief in Wicca. However, if a soul has reincarnated, the ancestor might not be offered for counsel.

CHAPTER FIVE

The Wheel of the Year

The Wiccan year is not the same as the standard Gregorian calendar, which begins on January 1st. Instead, it follows the four seasons, marking the development in the Earth's path around the Sun (which appears, of course, to be the Sun's journey around the Earth) and the corresponding changes to life in the world. Wicca has eight significant holidays, or Sabbats, 4 of which are "solar holidays": Summer Solstices and the Winter, and the Spring and Autumn Equinoxes. The other four Sabbats, or the "Earth celebrations," take place near the "cross-quarter days" in between the solar vacations, and are based on older pagan folk festivals which are believed to have been connected to the life process of animals and farming.

Keep in mind: The dates for the solar Sabbats are offered as a range to account for distinctions in the Sun's position in the sky relative to where one lives. The seasonal names for the Solstices and Equinoxes, as well as the seasonal associations with each Sabbat, are likewise different in the Southern Hemisphere.

The existence of 8 Sabbats, rather than four, acknowledges that the contemporary delineations we mark between "the four seasons" are somewhat artificial. For instance, Spring does not all of a sudden become Summer on June 21st; it has been relocating that instructions for a long time before the modern calendar acknowledges it as "Summer.".

An old name for the Summer Solstice is actually "Midsummer," acknowledging that Summer has been well underway by the time the Sun reaches its zenith in the sky. The cross-quarter Sabbats mark the "seasons in-between seasons" and assist the ongoing transitions along the Wheel of the Year. The Sabbats are thought about "days of power" and are marked by Wiccans, Witches, and other Pagans of lots of customs.

The Sabbats

• **Winter Solstice (Yule): December 20-23**

Considered in most Wiccan customs to be the beginning of the year, the Winter Solstice is a celebration of the rebirth of the God. It is the shortest day of the year, providing a welcome pointer that even though the cold season is still only getting underway, it doesn't last forever, as the days will begin to extend once again after this point. Some consider the first Full Moon after the Solstice to be the most powerful of the year. This is a joyful holiday commemorating light, in addition to preparation for a time of peaceful, inner focus as the Earth rests from her labor.

Amongst many Wiccans, the vacation is more frequently called "Yule," a name obtained from midwinter celebrations commemorated by Germanic people. "Yule" is still referenced in modern Christmas carols, and much of the traditions surrounding the Christian vacation, such as wreaths, Christmas trees, and caroling, have their roots in these older traditions. It was common for the Christian churches to "adopt" pagan vacations, repurposing them for commemorating saints or essential occasions, as a way of drawing individuals away from the Old Religion.

- **Imbolc: February 2**

Imbolc marks the first stirrings of Spring, as the long months of Winter are almost previous. The Goddess is beginning her healing after the birth of the God, and the extending days signify the conditioning of the God's power. Seeds start to germinate, daffodils appear, and hibernating animals begin to emerge from their slumber. It is a time for ritual cleansing after a long duration of inactivity. Covens may perform initiation rites at this time of new beginnings.

The name "Imbolc" is stemmed from an Old Irish word utilized to describe the pregnancy of ewes and has been, in some cases, translated as implying "ewe's milk" in referral to the birth of the very first lambs of the season. It is also called "Candlemas," and sometimes "Brigid's Day" in Irish customs. Linked with beginnings of development, it's considered a festival of the Maiden.

- **Spring Equinox (Ostara): March 20-23**

At the Spring Equinox, dark and light are lastly equal again, and development accelerates as both the light from the still-young God of the Sun and the fertility of the Earth grow more powerful. Gardening begins in earnest, and trees send blossoms to participate with the pollinating bees. The equal length of day and night produces time for balancing and bringing opposing forces into consistency.

The name "Ostara" comes from the Saxon Eostre, the Goddess of Spring and renewal. This is where the name Easter originates from, as this is another holiday that was "combined" with the Christian tradition.

- **Beltane: May 1**

As Spring begins to move into Summer, the Goddess begins making her transition into the Mother aspect, and God matures into his full effectiveness. Beltane is a fire celebration, and an event of recreation, love, and sex. It's at this time that the Goddess couples with God to ensure his renewal after his death at the end of the life process. Fertility is at its height, and the Earth prepares to thrive with new life.

The name "Beltane" comes from an ancient celebration commemorated throughout the Celtic Isles that marked the beginning of Summer, and is derived from an old Celtic word meaning "bright fire." The ancient Irish would light considerable fires to purify and protect their livestock, and jumping over fires was thought about a way to increase fertility and luck in the coming season.

• Summer Solstice/ Midsummer: June 20-23

Long thought about one of the most magical periods of the year, the Summer Solstice regards the Goddess and the God at the peak of their powers. The Sun is at its highest level, and the days are at their longest. This is a celebration of the abundance of sunshine and heat, and the physical symptom of wealth as the year heads toward the first of the harvests. It's a time of ease and short rest after the work of planting and before the work of harvesting begins. Some customs call this Sabbat "Litha," a name traced back to an old Anglo-Saxon word for this time of year.

• Lammas: August 1

Lammas signifies the beginning of the harvest season. The very first crops are generated from the fields, the trees and plants start dropping their fruits and seeds, and the days are growing shorter as the God's power begins to subside. This is a time for providing thanks for the abundance of the growing season as it begins to wind down.

The word Lammas comes from an old Anglo-Saxon word pairing meaning "loaf mass," and it was traditional to bless fresh loaves of bread as a method of celebrating the harvest. Lammas is at the same time called "Lughnasa," after the famous festivals in Ireland and Scotland held at this time to honor the Celtic god Lugh, who was connected with the Sun.

- **Fall Equinox (Mabon): September 20-23**

The harvest season is still in focus at the Autumn Equinox. The animals born during the year have grown, and the trees are starting to lose their leaves. Preparations are produced in the coming winter season. The God is making his exit from the real airplane and heading toward his mythical death at Samhain, and his supreme renewal at Yule. Then again, the nights and days are of equal length, signifying the short-term nature of all life, no season lasts permanently, and neither light nor dark ever overpowers the other for long. As with the Spring Equinox on the opposite side of the Wheel, balance is a style at this time.

The Autumn Equinox is thought about in some traditions to be "the Second Harvest," with Lammas as the first and Samhain as the last of 3 harvests. A more current name for the holiday is "Mabon," after a Welsh mythological figure whose origins are linked to a magnificent "mother and child" pair, echoing the dual nature of the relationship between the Goddess and the God.

- **Samhain: October 31**

Thought about by many Wiccans to be the most crucial of the Sabbats, Samhain is the time when the part death plays in the cycle of life is acknowledged and honored. The word "Samhain" originates from old Irish and is believed by numerous to mean "Summer's end." However, others trace it to a root word significance "assembly," which may describe the joint event of a pagan festival, particularly during the harvest season. As the Sun aspect, God retreats into the shadows as night starts to control the day. As the God of the Hunt, he is a pointer of the sacrifice of life that keeps us alive through the long winter season. The harvest is complete, and the sacred nature of food is appreciated. Amongst some traditions, this is viewed as the "Third Harvest."

Other and Wiccan pagan traditions view Samhain as a point in the Wheel when the "veil" in between the spiritual and material worlds is at its thinnest, and the days around Samhain are considered exceptionally reliable for divination activities of all kinds. Forbears are honored and interacted with at this time. A number of the Halloween traditions still celebrated in contemporary cultures today can be traced back through the centuries to this festival. Pagans of the old times left food offerings for their forefathers, which became the modern-day custom of trick-or-treating. Jack-o-lanterns developed from the practice of leaving candle-lit hollowed-out root veggies to direct spirits checking out in the world.

Some Wiccans in the Celtic customs think about Samhain, rather than Yule, to be the beginning of the year, as the death and rebirth aspects of production are seen to be inherently joined together-- death opens the space for new life to take root. Honoring the ancient Celtic view of the year having a "light half" and a "dark half," their Wheel of the Year starts once again on this day, the first day of the dark half of the year.

- **The Esbats**

In addition to the Sabbats, the Wiccan year consists of 12 (sometimes 13) Full Moon celebrations, known as the Esbats. While the Sabbats tend to focus event on the God and his association with the Sun, the Esbats honor the Goddess in her association with the Moon. Covens traditionally satisfy on the Esbats to celebrate a particular element of the Goddess, such as Aphrodite, in the event of abundance, or Persephone, in a routine for renewal. They work with the Goddess to bring about recovery and assistance for their communities and members, and frequently work for the good of the full world.

The Full Moon is also seen within the context of the Wheel of the Year, with names and seasonal attributions for each. For Wiccans dealing with specific elements of the Goddess, the particular goddess called upon during an Esbat will frequently correspond with the time of year. For example, Aphrodite is an appropriate goddess to celebrate abundance under a Summer Moon. In contrast, Persephone, with her underworld associations, is better suited to work with under a late Autumn or early Winter Moon.

The names for each Moon might vary from custom to custom; however, they are usually related to the time of year and the corresponding level of abundance and activity of life in the world, along with the Sun's point in its journey around the Earth. In the Northern Hemisphere, the most common names for the Full Moons in Wiccan routines are as follows:

Month	Moon Name
January	Cold Moon (also Hunger)
February	Quickening Moon (also Snow)
March	Storm Moon (also Sap)
April	Wind Moon (also Pink)
May	Flower Moon (also Milk)
June	Sun Moon (also Strong Sun and Rose)
July	Blessing Moon (also Thunder)
August	Corn Moon (also Grain)
September	Harvest Moon
October	Blood Moon
November	Mourning Moon (also Frost)
December	Long Nights Moon

Many Witches think about astrological influences in addition to seasonal influences and will work according to the specific sign the Moon is in while complete. They will describe the Moon appropriately, such as the "Gemini Moon" or the "Aquarius Moon."

If more than one Full Moon occurs in a given calendar month, it's called a Blue Moon. Happening roughly when every two and a half years, this is thought about an especially busy time in lots of Wiccan traditions, and individual attention is paid to working with the rare energy of a Blue Moon.

CHAPTER SIX

The Role Of Responsibility, Ethics, And Personal Connection With Deity

Wicca is more of a spiritual path. It is mostly concerned with the experience of the Divine and personal discovery. Wicca has no holy book or any written teaching that has been given through the ages for all Wiccans to follow. Wiccans develop their sacred texts of practices, lessons, spiritual experiences, and their understanding. Wicca doesn't have a hierarchy of leaders who counsel people on how to live and praise or those who ensure compliance with religious laws. Each Wiccan maintains a relationship with Deity, and each Wiccan acts as clergy.

Wiccans do have concepts and ethics that direct their behavior, and their objective is to stabilize personal freedom with obligation and regard for life's sacredness.

Building a Personal Relationship with the Divine

To self-directed people, Wicca is a wondrous and liberating venture. For people who want direction and structure in their spiritual lives, Wicca is not a great personal choice. This section checks out Wicca's absence of hierarchy and dogma and the encouragement of its strength, self-determination, individualism, and self-reliance.

Sending dogma to the doghouse

Individuals of many religions believe that Deity, usually referred to as God, is transcendent. Because people can't trust their natures, religious rules inform individuals what to do. Spiritual dogma defines the laws, mentors, beliefs, and concepts of religious beliefs, along with the consequences of breaking the laws. The laws and rules, like God, rise, separate from the world. They are infallible and undeniable. People should follow the laws and regulations, despite the personal expense.

Religious dogma and authority eliminate a person of the obligation of choosing on his or her actions. People abide by the spiritual power because they believe that the institution understands more, is more powerful, and is less likely to be corrupted than the person. They admit that the leaders in the institution can be relied on to know God's will.

Wiccans don't see themselves as different from a Deity. Their Goddess and/orGod is both transcendent and immanent. That implies that Deity is all present on the planet. People originate from and belong to the Divine energy, and the Deity is within everybody. Divine being is a supernatural innovative idea and action; but also remains connected to that creation. Wiccans think that they have a direct relationship with Divinity. They interact with the Goddess and the God themselves, and they do not require dogma or spiritual authorities to manage their frame of mind or direct their will or habits.

Wicca varies from many of the mainstream religions because it does not have a central authority with different levels of clergy who make or propound rules for all of Wicca. Whether the government acknowledges, the Wiccan clergy differs by the regional laws and whether the clergyperson seeks out such acknowledgment. Recognized clergy hold no unique location as part of some centralized religious body that supervises the Craft. Instead, Wicca is comprised of loosely linked and independent, little groups that specify their own spiritual beliefs and practices.

A lot of these little, independent groups do have leadership. The leaders supply assistance and instructions, but they generally don't exercise control over members. Wiccans separately choose how to think and practice.

Many small groups (called covens) have High Priests and Priestesses, or leaders with some different titles, who render their skills to the group and control its activities. Many Wiccan groups have levels of initiation; people advance as they grow and study in the Craft. Some of the groups have a Council of Elders who provide ongoing wisdom gotten during their long experience in the Craft. Nevertheless, in Wicca, leaders do not have control over others.

If a leader has proven experience, offers essential suggestions, and provides needed abilities, the group respects him or her and cooperates voluntarily. Still, nobody in Wicca is obligated to follow the leader.

Every Wiccan is seen as a Priest or Priestess. Each is considered to be clergy because they have direct access to Deity. Wiccans are expected to control or direct their own spiritual lives.

Doing the Right Thing: Ethics and Obligation

One of the most significant charges against the Craft is that it has no morality. Wiccans often are viewed as immature "if it feels great, do it" types who decline to follow the customs of good and decent folk. That's simply not true. Wiccans have a strong sense of ethics, and a brief trip to most Wiccan Websites shows that Wiccans spend a lot of time quibbling about the subtleties of principles and specific duty. Wiccans care a lot about what is wrong, and why. They generally are great people, but the basis for their policies is different from most traditional faiths.

Lots of Westerners see Deity as transcendent, as over and above the world. Human beings are separate from God, and they are independent of each other. People turn to spiritual dogma and organizations to help them live and analyze God's will.

Wiccan belief is quite different. The following concepts are significant to Wiccan practice:

People are connected in an interdependent circle or web of life. Because people are linked to each other, rather than separate, a Wiccan understands that doing damage to others eventually triggers damage to himself or herself.

Those concepts are the basis for the Wiccan Rede and the Threefold Law, which are the heart of Wiccan principles.

Following the Wiccan Rede

The eight words of the Wiccan Rede are; "And it harm none, do what ye will."

These words are the primary ethic of Wicca, referred to as the Wiccan Rede. The name rede indicates counselor recommendations. Some Wiccans think that the Wiccan Rede has been passed down through history. Some believe that it stemmed from Gerald Gardner.

Despite its origins, most Wiccans try to follow the Wiccan Rede, sometimes called simply "the Rede," and consider it to be the helping principle for their lives.

Following the Rede implies carrying out your own will, but acting in ways that trigger the least damage to yourself, others, the Earth, and all humans.

Wiccans generally analyze the Rede to mean that a Wiccan must "live and let others live, while appreciating the sacredness of all life. They need to think seriously about the effects of their actions before they act. Many Wiccans have broadened the scope of the Rede. They feel that apathy, disregard, and failure to work, to stop violence, abuse, suffering, or injustice, also breaches the Rede in some way.

Wiccans have the belief that life as a whole embodies Deity; Deity is all-present on the planet. To trigger damage to anything or anybody is to act contrary to the demands of the God and Goddess.

Following the Rede makes it a little complicated, though. It advises Wiccans not to cause harm to anyone. What about scenarios when a Wiccan is in the form of danger? Are Wiccans permitted to safeguard and protect themselves, even if they need to harm an enemy? Can a Wiccan protect or secure a family or neighborhood? Should a Wiccan damage one individual to save another person? What about cases when a severe injustice is causing lots of people to be harmed? Should a Wiccan action in and assist, possibly causing harm to a single person or group for the higher good of the community? Or should the Wiccan refuse to damage anyone and let wickedness go unchecked? Do Wiccans violate the Rede if they consume (and, therefore, harm) animals? Ask these questions at a Wiccan event and view the mix of emotions.

Wicca isn't simple—people practicing the craft deliberate seriously on these crucial questions.

They are accepting the consequences: The Threefold Law.

You might be familiar with the science of turmoil theory and the butterfly result. The concept behind the method is that all of life is a complicated system. A little change at one place in the network can lead to a significant impact somewhere else.

Everything that exists is connected, and any action, no matter how small or insignificant impacts everything else.

Negative or harmful energy not just hurts the target of the power, but the negativity and damage remain in nature's web and affect all of life, including the sender. For example, if individuals contaminate the Earth's water, ultimately, they need to drink harmful and contaminated water.

A Wiccan thinks that his/her energy is never different from the power of the rest of life and the universe.

Focusing on intent

This concept of interconnectedness is the basis for the other Wiccan ethic, the Threefold Law. Whatever an individual sends out returns threefold. Generally, the law means that whatever you do or say-- unfavorable or favorable, bad or excellent-- will go back to you with three times the intensity. Some Wiccans believe that this belief applies just to words and actions, but others consist of thoughts.

Whatever that exists becomes part of one unbroken circle. So when a Wiccan decide to send energy, especially deliberate, powerfully directed energy during magic, that individual's essence:

- remains in the Self
- forms part of the power being sent out.
- It is in the result-- the energy that takes a trip through the circle of life, nature's web, and ultimately goes back to the sender.

That's why this particular ethic is referred to as the Threefold Law. The concept is, in some cases, called the Law of Return.

Observing the hex caution.

Non-Wiccan media and society tend to concentrate on hexing and cursing whenever the topic of Wicca or Witchcraft shows up. The truth is that many Wiccans do not take part in hexing, cursing, and other unfavorable acts.

Many Wiccans do engage in binding and banishing. The meaning of these concepts are as follow:

- Binding: A Wiccan may cast a spell designed to restrict the actions or activities of someone.

- Banishing: A Wiccan may order someone (or some energy) to be gone. To banish means to send someone or something away-- from the area, or possibly, back to the source.

Since they are negative forms of magic, many Wiccans avoid these practices. Some Wiccans use binding and eliminating as last options, when somebody or something positions a severe danger, usually to the neighborhood (for instance, a group of Wiccans may choose to bind a crook whois victimizing others.

A lot of Wiccans are exceptionally unwilling to take part in any form of harmful magic since they understand that their energy is never different from the heat of other individuals, and causing harm to others eventually leads to damage to the Self. They also are conscious that the failure to act to stop violence, to relieve suffering, and to end oppression is an offense of noble task and a betrayal of the neighborhood. So making use of extraordinary power remains a constant challenge for people of the Craft.

The colors of magic.

You might hear some people explain different forms of magic by referring to colors. The most common references are made to white magic and black magic or light and dark magic. Most likely, the terms black and white or light and dark magic dates back to a time in ancient human history when the night or the dark was associated with danger and fear. The daytime or light implied safety. These labels emerged from folklore, not modern Wicca, and lots of Wiccans don't use these characterizations today.

Usage of these terms perpetuates stereotypes about the Craft. Using the words black magic and white magic enhances society's false information and fear about the nature of magic. Besides, when someone states that she or he is a "white" or "great" Witch or Wiccan, the difference implies that others are "black" or "bad" Wiccans and witches. Society does not identify the fans of mainstream religious beliefs in this way. For example, Methodists aren't asked to state whether they are white or black Methodists, or good or bad Methodists.

These labels have been around for a very long time, and if you continue to study Wicca, you will undoubtedly encounter them. Here's a basic description of the significances for the colors of magic:

White magic is carried out for a definite purpose, a favorable result, or spiritual growth. A person conducts magic for him/herself or for somebody who has an understanding of the charm and has provided consent without any kind of coercion. Some Wiccans may carry out white magic for an uninformed individual (for instance, somebody who is seriously ill). Nevertheless, in those cases, the professional makes a general ask for the best possible outcome and then sends the radiant energy to Deity or out into nature (instead of sending the magic directly to the uninformed individual)—a lot of Wiccanspractice the white magic type.

The Black magic is any type of magic that is performed to push someone into doing something; is targeted at somebody against his/her will; is intended at somebody without his/her knowledge; or is made use of to produce a restrictive, undesirable, unethical, or objectionable outcome. Wiccans do not knowingly practice black magic.

Gray magic is mostly situational, and Wiccans differ on the right principles of its usage. Gray magic incorporates all of the elements of white magic with an addition: Gray magic includes magic for defense or security of the Self or others from danger, crisis, abuse, or threat. Often it is magically provided for the higher good. Numerous Wiccans think that they commit to stop wickedness, that they can't ethically disregard abuse, suffering, injustice, and soon. Gray magic permits a reaction for the greater good.

Green magic has numerous meanings. The term often explains magic performed on behalf of nature, or to help the Earth and its inhabitants. It can likewise suggest magic for healing or to ensure health. In some cases, the term is used for magic done to produce prosperity and abundance.

Some Wiccans likewise refer to blue, red, yellow, orange, or purple magic, but the true meanings of these terms vary.

CHAPTER SEVEN

LivingWiccanToday

Wiccans may have some distinct practices, and they deal with some different challenges. However, the average Wiccan is a sharp contrast to the stereotypes that lots of people still hold. This chapter offers you a glimpse into Wiccan lives and answers the question, "What's it like to be Wiccan?"

Taking a Snapshot of Contemporary Wicca

Who are Wiccans? Media representations of Wiccans have become more considerate for many years. However, the TV and film images probably do not show the lives of average Wiccans.

In truth, no one truly knows how lots of Wiccans are, who they are, and what sort of lives they lead. Wicca does not have large institutions that can supply this aggregate information. Wicca is a spirituality of little, loosely linked groups (although the Internet may be changing that fact by reinforcing the Wiccan neighborhood). Wicca does not have organized leadership or a centralized organization.

Lots of people declare that Wicca is the fastest-growing religion in America; however, no difficult data exists to prove this claim. Studies by several non-Wiccan groups, the growth of the Wiccan presence on the World Wide Web, and the increase in Wicca-related book sales support the concept that the variety of Wiccans is increasing. Also, records suggest that attendance at Pagan festivals is high and probably growing. Celebrations are events that typically occur in a rural setting at the very same time each year. They usually last for a weekend, or maybe several days. Festivals differ in size, but some draw numerous individuals. They offer Pagans a chance to connect socially and to exchange details about beliefs and practices.

Common sense suggests that Wicca is altering in addition to growing. The early individuals in the Wiccan revival are now middle-aged, and numerous have children. Dr. Helen Berger argues that the participation of entire households motivates Wiccans to develop companies and churches that will assist Wicca to expand and endure as a religion. Dr. Berger recommends that Wiccan parents want the faith to be deemed genuine by society so that their kids won't suffer persecution for their beliefs. Nevertheless, keep in mind that the population of the Berger study was small (approximately 2,000 people from several customs, consisting of Wicca) and self-selected (significance that individuals were not randomly selected, and they volunteered to respond). These respondents might or may not represent Wicca as a whole.

Out of fear of persecution and desire for privacy, many Wiccans lead extremely low-profile lives. Numerous do not divulge their affiliation with Wicca to outsiders. They go to work or school. They get back, cook dinner, see some TV, and go to sleep. They participate in PTA conferences and little league video games. They go to the motion pictures. They do read lots of books—the average Wiccan appearances and lives practically like anybody else.

Keeping Silent or Telling the World: The Wiccan Dilemma

Some people carefully hide their beliefs and never inform others about their involvement in Wicca, not their families, not their good friends, and not even their employers. Such people hide their altars, keep their books hidden in drawers rather than displaying on racks, and discover a reason to leave in a rush when people start discussing religion. They just share their beliefs with like-minded Wiccans, and often without anyone at all.

Other individuals, from the minute they experience Wicca, begin informing everybody they understand about the fantastic new world that they have found. They stack books on their friends, they hang pentacles in their cubicles at work, and they wear vibrant T-shirts happily displaying their devotion to Wicca. They're happy, and they want the world to know it.

Both Of These Positions Have a Benefit.

People who keep quiet aren't merely being paranoid. Most of the Wiccans are well versed in the long and harsh history of persecution against real and supposed Witches. Discrimination and abuse continue today worldwide.

Some people desire to keep quiet since they stress over being put in a position where they are required to reveal the names of other Wiccans. Also, some Wiccans are alarmed by the escalating usage of technology to gather and expose personal information about people.

Quite reasonably, some Wiccans pick to limit the number of individuals who understand their faith and could cause the problem, or even put them in threat-- now or in the future. You should never ask someone directly whether he or she is a Wiccan or a Witch. Wait up until the info is offered. If a person mentions the topic in discussion, show that you are open-minded and responsive; however, wait on the person to confide in you. If others can hear your argument, and this advice goes double. Never, and I never suggest ever, "call out" anybody. Don't reveal to others that someone is Wiccan without very first getting approval in private. Please respect that some individuals wish to keep their religious beliefs to themselves.

Some Wiccans think about Wicca to be a mystery religion that must be kept secret from the public. A mystery religion is one wherein the Deity is exposed through individual experience. These occasions are concealed to preserve their power and significance. Likewise, according to this view, some things are the best-taught person to person and need not be revealed. Also, particular knowledge and strategies (magic, for instance) might be unsafe if used by individuals who have not had proper training or who might intend to hurt others.

Individuals who choose to freely share their beliefs also have some excellent factors for doing so. Individual empowerment, along with physical, emotional, and psychological strength, is common to Wicca. Some Wiccans feel that living in fear of discrimination or dispute is contrary to their beliefs and limits their capability to practice their religion. Being truthful and open about Wicca builds self- self-confidence, which in turn makes incredible work more reliable and makes the ritual more fulfilling.

Some Wiccans believe that keeping their spirituality concealed motivates persecution and puts Wiccans in more risk, not less. Numerous feel that rejecting their religion dishonors the Goddess and the God. They likewise think that silence dishonored the Witches and declared Witches who have been eliminated in the name of Witchcraft.

The majority of Wiccans, however, find themselves at a happy medium between these two extremes. Many share their beliefs with friends and family. A smaller number are open about their religious beliefs in the work environment. Everyone needs to determine his/her level of convenience.

Many individuals find Wicca to be liberating and joyous. In their enthusiasm for their brand-new religious beliefs, new Wiccans may be tempted to chatter on about their religion to anybody who will listen, without sizing up the situation or the individual.

Some Wiccan traditions encourage that newbies learn and train for 'a year and a day' before disclosing their participation in Wicca to their communities. (A day and a year is a current period in Wicca. The year-and-a-day method is to make sure that Wiccans prepare well and think about all effects before making significant changes in their lives.).

Spilling the magic beans to friends and family.

Although Wicca has its roots in ancient times and is older than many of the world's religious beliefs, the Wiccan revival is a reasonably current phenomenon. A lot of individuals practicing Wicca today were not born into religious beliefs. They come from the recognized mainstream religious beliefs, typically from Christianity. When.

Relative might feel dissatisfied, upset, betrayed, or terrified. In all fairness, these intense emotions are reasonable. The household may think that the new Wiccan has turned his or her back on God, and might now remain in danger of going to Hell or suffering other exiles from God, as well as being separated from the remainder of the household after death and for all of eternity.

Everyone can practice whatever faith satisfies his/her needs, and friends or family should bully no one. Brand-new Wiccans can ease their shift by attentively considering the question of who to tell about their interest in or dedication to-- Wicca. Everyone's neighborhood is various, with varying degrees of tolerance. Nevertheless, the following ideas might be helpful to a Wiccan who wishes to share his or her spirituality:

Be selective and use profundity. Telling your partner, your sibling, and your buddy about your interest or involvement in Wicca may be essential to you, but do you genuinely need to have the same discussion with your judgmental but frail 91-year-old grandpa, with whom you go to once a year at the retirement home 1,100 miles away?

Be clear about your motives. Why are you informing a specific friend or member of the family? Do you wish to be genuine and deepen your intimate bond with this individual? Or are you merely trying to shock or be defiant? The previous is an excellent reason; the latter is, maybe, immature.

Beware. People can be unpredictable. When I made my change in spirituality, a few of the individuals whom I believed would be hostile or afraid ended up being incredibly tolerant. Others, sometimes individuals I expected to be helpful, or a minimum of cute were unpleasant, cynical, or downright nasty. Know that if you reveal your involvement in Wicca, you run the danger of alienating people who are necessary to you.

Weigh the threats of disclosure against what you stand to gain. If you decide to talk about your spirituality, pick the moment sensibly. Do not talk about the issue during a crisis. Select a time when you are calm and unhurried. You might even wish to compose down what you want to say so that you can provide your beliefs and without stress and anxiety. Focus on the favorable and attempt to alleviate the other individual's worries and concerns. Be respectful of his/her opinions; however, remain clear about the truth that you have every right to pick your faith.

Venturing out: Wicca in the work environment.

Choosing whether to be open about Wicca in the office is a huge choice that can have significant monetary repercussions. If you are checking out Wicca or have made a dedication, think of the benefits and drawbacks of divulging your beliefs before you speak about your spirituality at your worksite. You will most likely find that the novelty subsides quickly, and co-workers will treat you the same as they continuously have. Be mindful of the potential disadvantage of coming out of the broom closet at work. Here are some examples of bad things that can take place to good Wiccans:

Well, this one is apparent: You can get fired. Even in places where laws and business policies protect freedom of faith in the office, an employer who has strong opinions against Wicca might end you and mention other factors. Even if your immediate supervisor is open-minded and tolerant, your manager's boss might not be. Or the boss's discrimination might be more subtle. You may be passed over for promos or find your work under more examination. In some cases, you could submit a lawsuit; however, legal recourse is pricey, time-consuming, and seldom successful.

If you are in a service or an occupation that makes you dependent on clients or customers for your livelihood, understand that any disclosure about Wicca might threaten your sales or your relationships with clients. Depending on the nature of your service and your location, you might end up being the target of a boycott.

Be prepared to deal with co-workers who try to transform you. Other individuals may be interested and want to speak about your beliefs. Some of these conversations might be remarkably pleasant. Others might not be.

On the flip side, you may discover that a few of your colleagues avoid you, or perhaps avoid you. Associates may display hostility or worry. Depending on your office, the stigma might be long-term or temporary.

Wiccans-- specifically women-- have been stereotyped as being sexually promiscuous, uninhibited, and unrestrained. Whether this uses to you or not, the assumption can trigger issues at work in the kind of unwanted advances and even harassment.

The Benefits Of Being Open About Your Spirituality:

However, the scenario isn't all bad. The following are a few of the benefits of being open about your spirituality:

Some employers enable Wiccans the very same privileges as individuals of other faiths. Your employer might let you take off time on Wiccan holy days. Or you can work out for crucial days off; for example, you can offer to cover for your colleague on Good Friday if your colleague takes your place on Beltane.

You don't need to lie or avoid discussions that involve religion or spirituality. In a workplace where individuals are close and frequently share info about their personal lives, lying about or concealing your beliefs can get messy and tiresome.

When people know someone who is Wiccan, they are less most likely to think and promote stereotypes about Wiccans. Being open enables you to construct excellent will for Wicca and lead the way for others if you act morally and honorably.

Living outside of the mainstream needs guts. Having the stability, to be honest about your beliefs and face personal attacks can be empowering. The strength and self-confidence that you develop can serve you well in other areas of your life.

Wicca motivates individuals to live their lives with courage and stability. The next section offers a take a look at the sometimes distinct Wiccan approach to life and its passages.

Dancing the Circle of Life: Wiccan Passages.

Like everybody else, Wiccan lives are differentiated by passages: birth, adolescence, falling in aging, death, and love. Like individuals of every religion and culture, Wiccans engage in rituals, events, and rites to mark these happy or solemn celebrations. The following areas describe how Wiccans come and distinguish to terms with life's remarkable minutes.

Naming or Wiccaning of a child.

When a child comes into a Wiccan household, by birth or adoption, Wiccans might hold a ceremony to call the kid and place her or him under the protection of the Goddess and God, as well as the Wiccan community. The vast majority of Wiccans do not consider this to be a commitment or initiation of the kid into Wicca. It is more of an open event. The routine is simple and ordinarily short; however, it varies according to tradition. Non-Wiccans are generally complimentary to go to. Usually, a Priestess or Priest commands the ritual. Often a circle is cast. The rite typically includes the list below elements (the order might differ):.

- The kid is welcomed. He or she exists or presented to the Deity and the community.
- The kid is given his/her name.
- The selected Deity is asked to protect and bless the child.
- The community is asked to bless the child and safeguard. In some cases, each witness to the rite offers a one-sentence true blessing
- .The kid might be shown images of the forefathers, and the ancestors might be asked to bless the kid. The kid might be introduced to living relatives.
- All the guests take pleasure in wine (or juice) and cakes.

The rite ends, and the event is frequently followed by a party with feasting and the opening of gifts for the child. The Naming event is to show love and assistance for the kid and his or her household and is usually a warm and pleasing event.

Marking adolescence.

Coming-of-age rites that mark the age of puberty are not a universal practice in Wicca. Just like the rest of society, not all Wiccan moms and dads are entirely comfy with their kids' advance into sexual maturity, and adolescents might be too shy or ashamed to want this kind of event.

The rite is ending up being more typical for ladies. Some Wiccan women arrange rites of passage for their daughters in an attempt to balance the negative cultural conditioning that girls get about their bodies. For example, lots of young ladies are taught directly or indirectly that menstruation is a curse and a penalty for evil. No set structure exists for these coming-of-age rites, but most have the following in typical:

- For a lady, the rite generally occurs after she has her first menstruation. For a boy, the time is less plainly specified; however, it is usually around the time his voice deepens, and he starts to grow body hair.
- The rites haven't typically deemed a devotion or an initiation into Wicca. The age that kids reach puberty generally is thought about too young to make an educated life choice about religious beliefs.
- Guests are all of the very same sex as the teen going through the rite.
- The young individual understands about the rite ahead of time and understands the significance. Typically, she or he has the chance to take part in the preparation.

- Throughout the rite, the girl or young male is invited into adulthood and provided to the Goddess and/or God.

- Both pride and responsibility are worried during the ceremony.

- Typically, specific attendees offer brief little bits of recommendations to the adolescent.

- In some cases, the young adult is asked to symbolically part with some item from childhood, and after that, she or he is given something to represent the entry into adulthood. For some Wiccan families, this event is when the young person gets his or her first routine tools.

Aging with dignity: The wisdom of the Crone and Elder

One of the terrific disasters of modern-day civilization is how we treat the old. In this culture, individuals are valued based on their performance; that is, what they add to the system. The result is that children and the old are frequently cheapened and disrespected. Wiccan values reach back to the perfects of an earlier time, when all people had intrinsic worth, and the former were valued and respected.

Wiccans carry out Croning or Eldering rites to honor older members of the Craft who have acquired understanding, ability, and wisdom. To many in the Craft, an Elder is a guy or a woman who has reached his or her late 50s or older. Many Wiccans consider retirement age to be the time for an Eldering event. The term Crone typically applies to a female who has reached menopause. Crone is a regard to regard, not scorn. It is also the term for the 3rd aspect of the Goddess (Maiden, Mother, and Crone).

Croning or Eldering rituals are uncommon. The Wiccan revival wasn't fully underway up until the 1950s, so the number of older individuals in the Craft is restricted. As the Wiccan population ages, this ritual probably will end up being more prevalent.

Croning and eldering are rites of celebration and recognition. The focus is not just on the past accomplishment, however likewise the future capacity of the Elder or Crone.

Like coming-of-age rites, no set structure exists for this type of ritual. The celebration is geared to the person. Usually, a circle is a cast, and a Priest, Priestess, or other members of the community accompanies the Elder or Crone into the ring and presents him or her to the group of guests. The person's life and contributions are summarized. Frequently the Elder/Crone is given a gift signifying the celebration. Visitors are welcomed to speak, and after that, the Elder/Crone deals with the group. Celebration and gift-giving often follow the routine.

CHAPTER EIGHT

Wiccans Dealing with death

Everything in life, whatever in the cosmos, is made from one unbroken and eternal circle of energy. Energy has no start and no end. It can be changed, but it can not stop to exist. Truth is in ideal balance, a simultaneous cycle of creation and damage and birth, re-creation and death, and rebirth. This pattern repeats throughout the natural world, from the smallest of cells to the most huge of stars; everything is in an endless cycle of regeneration. The majority of Wiccans think that the very same concept holds real for human lives, and reincarnation is one of the most commonly held beliefs in Wicca.

Some Wiccans believe that after enough lifetimes or incarnations, the soul will reach a state of perfection and go back to the Divine Source.

Wiccans have varied concepts about the afterlife, and some are complicated. Some viewpoints take into account that time is not direct, and individuals might be living numerous lives at when. Some belief in Oversouls that branch off and manifest in multiple physical lives. Regardless of the subtleties, the majority of Wiccans do think in reincarnation.

Wiccans see death as a clean slate. They grieve similar to everybody else, but the unhappiness is from the pain of separation from the enjoyed one. If a Wiccan was open about his/her spirituality, the rites and the funeral service could be Wiccan, commanded by Wiccan clergy or a High Priestess or Priest. Wiccan memorial rituals differ according to custom, individual choice, and whether non-Wiccans exist. Usually, a circle is a cast, and the departed is kept in mind as in any considerate memorial service. Lots of Wiccans define that they desire to be cremated after death. However, Wiccans may pick various burial choices.

Ideally, the Wiccan has made arrangements for the disposal of his or her spiritual home, such as tools and the Book of Shadows. These individual

items might be damaged, buried with the Wiccan, or passed on to household or pals in the Craft. Fellow coveners or Craft pals should make sure that familiars and animals of the departed get a great house. (A familiar is an animal who has a psychic bond with a Wiccan.).

Infighting in the Witch Wars.
Wicca is in transition. It's acquiring legitimacy in the eyes of the general public. More Wiccans are venturing out of the broom closet and reaching out to one another. By all indications, Wicca is growing hugely. Wiccans are residing in a time of development and celebration of dialogue and exchange. The Goddess is re-emerging, and the world is rosy and bright for individuals of the Craft.

If you invest more than 10 minutes online going to Wiccan or Pagan Web websites, you'll see references to the Witch Wars.

The term is a little frightening and motivates stereotypical images of Witches hurling curses and lightning bolts at one another or Witches lined up on the field of battle, using middle ages garb and wielding long, decorated swords. This is not the case. The current Witch Wars are wars of words, but they do get pretty awful.

What are the Witch Wars?

In general, a Witch War is a verbal Internet fight between two or more people who call themselves Wiccans or Witches that occurs frequently.

Witch Wars generally begin little, in between people or small groups. The conflict spreads by way of gossip through the community (this chatter is in some cases called bitchcraft or Wicca). When the dispute reaches the media (most typically the Internet) and involves others in the neighborhood, it acquires momentum. Wiccans frequently are strong-minded individuals who think critically about issues. As a dispute gains public attention, others include their viewpoints to the fray, which draws more attention and greater media participation, which attracts others into the argument, and so on, till the result is a full-blown Witch War.

Witch Wars begin in numerous ways, consisting of the following situations:

- A single person or group questions the legitimacy of another individual's or group's beliefs, practices, training, or motivations. These arguments generally start with words such as, "You aren't a genuine Wiccan since ..." (See the following area for more on bad terms, such as fluff bunny and white lighter.).

- A person or group has a bad experience with another individual or group. Numerous Witch Wars begin with disappointments in covens. In some cases, the factor is simply coven politics: arguments over belief and practice, struggles for power, and breakdowns of communication (the very same issues that happen in other groups in society). Sometimes, the charge is more dangerous. One individual accuses another (or the group) of violating Wiccan principles, for example, implicating a member of sexual misconduct.

- Whatever the issue, the concern gets vented in public, usually on the Internet, and individuals take sides. Individuals exchange spoken fire until the debate is dealt with or burns out, one of the individuals leaves the field, or cooler heads prevail.

Among the considerable aspects contributing to the environment that creates Witch Wars is that, so a couple of covens exist. Lots of people are so desperate to find a coven that they end up among individuals with whom they aren't suitable. Individuals are thrown up who might have extremely various views about essential problems, such as management, ritual nudity, and so on. From this mix comes a difference that ends up being public and then spreads until another Witch War is at full speed.

A leader's integrity is perceived to be compromised.

Individuals view a particular leader to be in the Craft for his/her ego rather than spiritual reasons, for example, to wield power over others, to enjoy the adulation of fans, to get publicity, or to earn money. The leader's followers defend him or her; others publicly attack; war starts.

Wiccans argue over money.

Frequently, these disputes have to do with: The quality or authenticity of goods, services, training, or triggers is in concern. Are the owners of the local Pagan book shop supporting the community or exploiting it? (The vast bulk are invaluable resources to the community. However, some aren't.) Should a local coven charge people for Wiccan training? Should Wiccans claim that they can recover, and charge for this service?

- Rival Wiccan or Pagan organizations contend for donations. There are many useful organizations and insufficient Pagan dollars to support them. (Before you contribute, evaluate any Wiccan or other Pagan company naturally as you would any other group. Request a financial declaration and ask a lot of questions. A lot of are happy to accommodate your items.).

- Wiccans disagree about a company's plan. For instance, they may argue about whether or not to spend the neighborhood's cash to take a local case of discrimination to court.

Wiccans remain in conflict about what is and is not ethical habits.

This category encompasses a variety of issues. When, if ever, should Wiccans use magic for defense or defense? Should a Wiccan make claims about his or her ability to heal? When, if ever, is attempting to repair somebody without his or her knowledge and consent proper? Should Wiccans charge money for recovery? Should Wiccans charge money to teach the Craft? What kind of magic is acceptable?

The Internet seems to change how Wiccans and other Pagans interact with one another. Communication on the Internet, in email, chatroom, newsgroups, Web sites, and so on, often is confidential. Individuals feel freer to vent their feelings straight, impulsively, and with less tact than they would use during an in-person encounter. Sadly for the Wiccan neighborhood, name-calling and dispute have ended up being widespread online.

Who are white lighters and fluff bunnies?

Name-calling appears to have been raised to an art form on the Web. Names such as play an, fluff bunny, and whitelighter-- are used with varying degrees of intensity, from light-hearted fun to deep hostility. The significances of the terms depend on who utilizes them and in what context.

People new to the Craft go online and expect to discover Wiccans who respect all beings and live by the Wiccan Rede "An' it harm none, do what ye will" (Doreen Valiente, Pentagram, Volume One, 1964, released by Gerard Noel). Instead, sometimes they find Wiccans requiring conformity and spitting venom at one another. I include this area, not to motivate or excuse the usage of these words; however, so that beginners aren't blindsided by these habits; therefore, they understand the many terms that are being bandied about.

Fluff and light

Fluffy bunny and highlighter are the most typical terms that you may see on Wiccan Web sites and in publications. Initially, these bad terms were used by Wiccans and other Pagans about the

New Age neighborhood. New Agers, in some cases, were deemed holding beliefs of little substance, and as being unrealistic, superficial, pointless, and, in many cases, materialistic. The paths of the New Agers, Wiccans, and other Pagans often crossed, and some

Wiccans and other Pagans rushed to separate themselves from what they considered as New Age fad. When the name-calling began, that's. The terms slowly progressed and were more often directed at Wiccans, whom others in the neighborhood felt were being New Age in their beliefs or practices.

A fluffy bunny or fluffy bunny is someone who is embracing or exploring Wicca for the wrong factors or in the incorrect methods, according to his or her critics. The term generally refers to individuals who do not understand or investigate the history, beliefs, or procedure that underlie the practice of Wicca. For some, Wicca is a trend; for others, it's a type of rebellion against society, the federal government, parents, or a mainstream church. Some are drawn into the tools, clothes, fashion jewelry, spells, public image, or media buzz; however, they have little interest in spiritual development. Some concentrate on particular misconceptions or assumptions about Wicca and hold simplistic or biased views about Wicca and its history. Some are blindly devoted to one author or leader, however never research study and investigate further to get a deeper or wider point of view on the Craft. Some learned their

Craft by watching popular television programs, such as Charmed, Sabrina the Teenage Witch, or Buffy the Vampire Slayer. All these folks have lots of fluff, according to their critics. (Playgan, rhymes with Pagan, is another term utilized for individuals who don't seem to take their Craft Seriously.).

A highlighter, a term in some cases utilized interchangeably with fluff bunny, is somebody for whom imagining white light (hence the name, highlighter) and sending good energy are enough for the practice of Wicca and the enhancement of the world. Whitelighters do not desire to take obligation for achieving particular acts in the Craft, typically because they don't wish to run the risk of doing any harm. They do not explore how Craftworks. They concentrate on joyous and positive routine, and mainly disregard significant issues worldwide. This term explains feel-good, delighted Wicca combined with New Age philosophy and practiced by people who don't have a clue, according to the critics who use this term.

The definitions of these terms vary, depending upon the context and the critic, but they are rarely used as a favorable or encouraging comment. (However, the unfavorable significance of whitelighter might be altering because of the popularity of the tv show, Charmed. On that program, a highlighter is a spiritual protector or guardian, and that meaning is working its way into general use.).

Sticks and stones.

The preceding are primary descriptions for these disparaging words. Their use has become much more widespread and isn't restricted to those descriptions. Wiccans often snap with these words in the following situations:

More knowledgeable members of the Craft judge the sincerity or integrity of new Wiccans or people exploring Wicca.

Some Wiccans and other Pagans call every newcomer a fluff bunny. (A a little more helpful term for someone new to Wicca or Paganism is newbie; the more respectful and respectful name is hunter.).

The generation space often fuels this division in the Craft. Older Wiccans usually charge that the younger ones just don't understand what times resembled when Wicca was harmful, deceptive, and hard to gain access to. The older generation developed modern-day Wicca in a world that was hostile to them, and some are afraid that the more new age will make modifications in the traditions that they worked so tight and risked a lot to develop. Some do not think that young Wiccans value the severity of the course. Members of covens (arranged little groups) judge solitaries.

(Wiccans who practice alone).

Many traditions (denominations or sects) of Wicca do not recognize as legitimate individuals who practice Wicca without being and joining a coven started into a formal custom, slowing Wicca's emergence as a spirituality that society recognizes as genuine. Witch Wars and name-calling enhance society's stereotypes of Wiccans as possibly dangerous individuals without any morals and principles.

If such internal disputes continue, efforts to get acceptance for Wicca in the courts, the workplace, and other institutions will take longer. It also implies that the children of Wicca are most likely to grow up dealing with persecution, discrimination, and public hostility instead of progressive approval.

The Wiccan community can, and does, interact to further shared objectives. Most Wiccans welcome new specialists and are more than willing to listen to others and discuss their own beliefs in a non- confrontational way. The secret for Wiccans is to transport the passion into enhancing the Craft, not into protecting specific positions or assaulting those of others.

CHAPTER NINE

Considering The Wiccan Path

Some Wiccans know intuitively that Wicca is best for them. From the beginning, they never question their choice of spiritual path. Others have a more analytical nature, and they analyze their religious decisions. Vigilance and uncertainty are very welcome in Wicca. Wicca supports questioning of authority.

Looking Inward

Many people have chosen to read this book just because they want information about Wicca and Witchcraft. If that's true for you, this area does not personally apply. If you mean to pursue a much more in-depth exploration of Wicca or you're moving towards making a dedication, make sure that you aren't drawn to Wicca for reasons that are unrelated to faith. If it is followed for purposes other than spiritual ones, the Wiccan knowledge will not be gratifying or transforming. If your response to any of the following questions is yes, take a while to reconsider your interest in Wicca:

1. Is somebody pressuring you to get involved in?

Wicca?

Wiccans support independence, free choice, and personal strength. They do not attempt to convert others. If somebody is trying to push you into participating in Wiccan activities or study, that individual is not a real Wiccan, and you may have to free yourself from such manipulation.

2. Are you angry at your previous religion, and you think that Wicca is the"opposite" of your former faith?

Many injustices have been done in the name of or under the guise of religion. Naturally, some people feel betrayed by religious organizations. You will be more efficient if you choose a religion for positive and genuine reasons.

3. Are you drawn to Wicca just because you view it to be counter-cultural, underground, or subversive?

The reality is that Wicca can be considered worthy of all these labels. However, Wicca is foremost and first a spirituality, not merely a method to rebel against your household, the government, or mainstream society.

4. Do you feel lonely and think that Wicca, specifically a coven, can function as a family and satisfy your requirements for companionship?

Many coveners do develop strong, close-knit bonds with one another. A reverence for Deity and a love of nature, not a desire to fulfill emotional needs, are the basis for a sound dedication to Wicca.

By the way, Wiccans do not cut their ties to household and good friends when they commit themselves to Wicca. They continue to support their relationships with individuals beyond Wicca.

5. Are you in the real sense, just searching for sex?

The concept that Wiccans and Witches engage in orgies as part of their rites is prevalent. This stereotype isn't real; sexual activity is not a part of standard Wiccan practice.

6. Are you brought in just to the image or the more remarkable aspects of Wicca, for instance, jewelry, robes, tools, or fancy routines?

The practice of Wicca is gorgeous, but the basis for Wiccan activities is to honor the Deity and commemorate the natural world.

7. Do you think that Wicca can provide you some secret power or details that can solve your problems, such as getting you out of debt, breaking an addiction, or healing your relationship with your partner?

The majority of people understand that it's not possible to point a finger or wiggle a nose to clean up your home right away, attract a mate, or conquer enemies. Some people do have the idea that Wicca can impart a secret power or expose some unearthly ancient knowledge.

It is a fact that Wicca is a spirituality of profound knowledge; its roots remain in the Old Religion, which reaches back countless years. Wicca can offer you tools for transforming your life (for example, details about healing or rituals for growth and empowerment).

It is also the truth that the practice of magic directs energy, which could enable you to make modifications in yourself and the world. However, nobody in Wicca can bestow upon you a word, beauty, or spell that unexpectedly puts an end to all your difficulties.

8. Speaking of television Witches, are you buying into the media buzz?

From Samantha to Sabrina to the siblings on Charmed, Witches have been continuously popular on television, but be assured that real-life Wicca isn't anything like television Witchcraft.

This section brings to light some nonreligious reasons that people might be brought in to Wicca and Witchcraft; the next article addresses some of the spiritual problems that people grapple with as they consider whether Wicca is ideal for them.

Asking the Big Questions.

How do individuals select their faiths? Some are born into a religion and never question their devotion to their childhood religious beliefs. Some claim to understand intuitively when they discover the religious beliefs or spirituality that is best for them. Others participate in a mission to find the perfect spiritual course. They discover their core values and concepts and then compare them to the mentors of different religions. The following are common or regular questions that people might ask themselves when they are attempting to define their beliefs:

- How do I wish to live? What is my purpose? What is most important to me?
- What type of interpersonal relationships do I desire to have?

- How do I wish to raise my children? How do I want to treat my
  parents?
- How do I desire to express my sexuality?
- How essential is money in my life? What am I happy to do to
  get it?
- What happens to me when I die? How do I prepare for death?
  Am I scared to die?
- How do I feel about the world? Do I desire to live fully in it?
  Change it? Escape it? Transcend it?
- How do I value other people around me?
- How should individuals treat the Earth?
- What is morality? What is evil? Does evil exist?
- Do I genuinely believe in a holy book or other doctrines?
- Who or what do I rely on when I am suffering?
- Do I believe in any Deity? How do I envisage Deity?

A lot of religions spell out the answers to these questions in
detail. They have at least one holy book that deals with these
problems. They also have churches or other organizations with
leaders who interpret doctrine and counsel people about how to
live.

Ideally, a person's core or significant values, beliefs, and principles agree with the mentors of his/her chosen faith, suggesting that he or she concurs with the religion's leaders and teaching.

Wicca does not have a teaching or holy book that Wiccans must follow, nor does it have leaders who require that people live a specific way. Wicca is a spiritual path with some core principles and objectives that most Wiccans hold in common. Their responses show the core concepts of Wicca when Wiccans address these huge life questions. Wiccans select this spiritual path since they share the standard Wiccan ideas about life, the world, and Deity.

Wiccan Principles

A Wiccan can decline several of the principles that a lot of Wiccans hold in common. No authority decides who is and is not a legitimate Wiccan. However, it's doubtful that someone can be pleased or reliable in Wicca if he or she declines the bulk of the following core principles:

- **Immanent Deity**

Practically all Wiccans think Creatively. Wiccans can have drastically different understandings of Deity. Many Wiccans define Deity in both the male and female aspects, that is, the Goddess and God. The principle of immanence is central to Wicca. Immanence implies that.

Divine being is right here, right now, and is all-present on the planet, instead of transcendent (over or beyond the world). People originate from and belong to the Divine energy, and Deity is within everyone. A Wiccan's crucial spiritual intent is to grow in his/her relationship with Divinity.

Interconnection

Wiccans believe that everything is interconnected. All of human existence is an unbroken circle of energy, and everything is combined into one living organism. Nature is a manifestation of Deity, and individuals commit to regard, safeguard, and protect the natural world.

Love for Community

For Wiccans, the word "community" incorporates all the natural world, consisting of all people. Since it is a manifestation of Deity, Wiccans feel an individual responsibility to respect and serve the community. It was harming, even by neglect or apathy breaches, Wiccan principles. Respecting and serving the community means working to end any condition that causes harm, consisting of poverty and oppression. Wealth ought to not be valued over people, the Earth, and its inhabitants. Sexuality is a symptom of and a gift from Divinity. Therefore it ought to be celebrated, taken part in carefully, and never used to cause damage.

Since Deity is within everybody, all people are equal, and they should not be seen differently based on race, ethnic culture, sex/gender, sexual preference, class, education, or beliefs. Wiccans are not perfect, and prejudice exists in Wicca, as in every other section of society. Still, bias breaches Wiccan principles and ethics, as does any type of violence or abuse.

Life and the afterlife.

Wiccans think that whatever that exists is an unbroken circle of energy. Energy has no beginning and no end. Life is a cycle of rebirth, birth, and death. Based on this conception, many Wiccans believe in some type of reincarnation, although the information differs. Lots of think that, upon death, the soul or the awareness goes to the Summerland, a location of peace and natural charm that is located in non-physical, non-ordinary reality. The soul or consciousness might rest in Summerland, review the life that has just passed, and decide whether to reincarnate or explore other possibilities.

Nearly all Wiccans agree that lifestreams from the Deity, so life is not to be simply endured or suffered. The Wiccan intent is to honor Divinity by living life to its fullest potential-- not to go beyond experience, but to revel in it.

Wiccan Ethics.

Wicca doesn't force individuals to abide by commandments and laws. The Threefold Law and the Wiccan Rede are widely accepted in Wicca. They are guidelines by which each Wiccan constructs his/her code of principles. Wiccans quibble amongst themselves about the nuances, nevertheless, if somebody thinks in general to the ethical requirements in this area, she or he most likely would not be comfortable in Wicca.

Self-direction and individual obligation

Wicca is a spirituality, not a religious belief. It is based on experience, not doctrine. No holy book or leader tells people what to do and when, or offers forgiveness for sin. Wiccans decide on an individual basis how to live, how to praise, and how to practice Wicca. Lots of people discover this lack of structure liberating; others might feel insecure and directionless.

Protection of personal privacy and restriction on proselytizing

Privacy and confidentiality are essential in Wicca. The individual chooses whether to be open about his/her spirituality and if and when to reveal such info. No one may expose the identity of another Wiccan. To do so could jeopardize the person's friendships, career, kid custody, and so on.

Wiccans do not proselytize (meaning that they don't try to convert others to their religious beliefs). They feel that proselytizing is unneeded; individuals who are drawn to Wicca look for and discover others of like mind.

Knowing for Sure

How does someone understand for sure whether he or she is Wiccan? If you ask Wiccans this question, you may get actions like these:

" I feel in my bones.".

" It seemed like I was coming home.".

" I feel the existence of the Goddess." "I got an indication from nature.".

These are all truthful actions, but they aren't efficient to somebody who is examining Wicca from the outside.

Since it is based on individual experience, Wicca is tough to get a handle on. Wicca is a spirituality of exploration and discovery, instead of church services and doctrine. Wiccans discover their connection to Deity. They feel the presence of, or they interact with, the Goddess and God. They start to feel a deep kinship with the universe. They may begin to pay attention to and discover significance in synchronicities (coincidental occasions that seem associated) occurring in their lives. Their understandings change, and they end up being conscious of nature's cycles and patterns. They typically find themselves gaining wisdom from the natural world, including animals.

Wiccans typically do not believe in coincidence. They live their lives open up to interaction from Deity and in tune with nature. Feeling the existence of Divinity and the bond with the natural world affirms their choice of Wicca as their spiritual course.

Taking the First Step

A lot of Wiccans would recommend that you don't hurry headlong into it if you feel drawn to Wicca. Your spiritual journey will be a lot more changing and fulfilling if you take some time and exercise your sensations and beliefs. Start gradually. Do you believe in the Goddess and God? Begin hoping regularly and support the Divine relationship.

Do not get caught up in attempting to work magic immediately. You might not get the wanted outcome if you do not build a structure of understanding.

Focus on natural phenomena, such as solar and lunar eclipses. Invest some time in nature and let yourself be completely present and open. Put ordinary fret about profession or household aside for a time, and concentrate on your environments. Feel the interconnection of all living things and the existence of the Goddess and the God. That is the very best possible intro to Wicca.

CHAPTER TEN

Principles Of Wiccan Belief

Like most real kinds of spirituality, Wicca creates complacency and stability within the follower. This sense of balance brings a guarantee for the future. When this sense of security is integrated with a real love for deity, the deep space of the soul is filled, and genuine assurance is found.

Among the most exceptional functions of all religious beliefs are beliefi.ebelief in deity, sacred bible, and ritual customs. Ideas form the nucleus of all spiritual systems. They are the source from which the faith thrives and grows. Without strong beliefs, no teaching can weather the tides of time.

Since Witchcraft is a child with lots of fathers and the offspring of a thousand complaints, it is hard to place the beliefs of one tradition above another. No one knows for sure where the majority of Wicca's doctrines come from, and to make complex matters, the majority of modern Wiccans often disagree when it comes to religious issues.

There is something that most Pagans and Wiccanswill agree on: The Principles of Wiccan Belief. These principles form the foundation of modern Wiccan belief, much as the Ten Commandments do for the Christian religion. The concepts, which follow, were embraced by the Council of American Witches at their 1974 spring meeting in Minneapolis. Many Wiccans still cling to these principles, although the council disbanded soon after its spring meet that year.

Conventional Coven Policy

The word "coven" generally summons visions of individuals all worn black, wildly dancing around a bubbling cauldron. While this picture is not always without merit, it is not the amount total of Witchcraft or the Wiccan religion.

Many Witches choose to stay solitary (that is, to work alone), some join covens, generally made up of thirteen individuals, including a leader. The number thirteen is considered lucky just because it can't be divided against itself. This is, however, the suitable, and not the norm. The majority of groups have far fewer members.

One of the very first things a new member is given upon signing up with a coven is a list of tenets or coven laws. The coven members have drafted these laws to maintain order. They are generally based upon an act of courtesy and common sense, two things many people appear to forget when feelings are involved.

The Laws

1. Each tradition or group in Wicca has its own processes and beliefs. Each must follow according to its path. So long as it hurts none and respects the spirit of deep space, all traditions will be considered as equally legitimate under the God and Goddess.

2. Our members believe there is a supreme force that created and maintained deep space and represented itself through the myriad of universal goddesses and gods. We acknowledge these

gods and goddesses as entire and complete unto themselves and equal unto each other.

3. On our part, we do not fear to have a lady bring in a female, nor a guy bring in a male. It is better to have a wise instructor of the same sex than a fool of the opposite.

4. We see Wicca as a response, not a reason to prevent that which takes effort or might be emotionally hurtful.

5. For those who look for the initiation, it must be kept in mind that the introduction is an occurrence within the heart. The ceremony is just its restatement before the gods and those who represent them.

6. Within any organization, there should be a leader or several leaders. In Wicca, we recognize that there is no such thing as an ideal High Priestess or High Priest. The imperfections of the leaders should not be the reason for a disorder, but rather for love, tolerance, and understanding.

7. When there should be a cessation of friendship, there comes a time in every family or coven. What one might avoid saying to a good friend or liked one, one may be forced to say as a High Priestess or High Priest. Discipline is one such responsibility.

8. You should remember you will never have the power of the instructor who tutored you. This does not mean that you won't

ever have the same amount of energy as those who came in the past.

Power is not an ability, and your capability may surpass all others. Power is the ability to demand respect. You will never have the regard due to your instructors. Need your own by controlling your ability.

9. Thinking of hurting is not like working to cause discomfort. Each step may be accomplished with little force of will, but with greater strength of will, both can be prevented.

10. Those with knowledge and capability need not show it—those who fear their ability to fear themselves. Worry has no location within the Craft of the Wise.

11. Express only that which you know. Work only within your world of schedule. Leave the fools unto themselves, and look for people with the truth in their hearts. Don't allow their words or actions lead you but instead, seek to their works and deeds.

12. Observe, listen, and reserve judgment. For till the silver is weighed, who knows the weight.

13. Always treat others as you would want to be dealt with. Keep in mind that evil begets evil, but good begets pleasure and joy.

CHAPTER ELEVEN

Deity: The God And Goddess

Wicca is an extremely individualized religion, in which each individual selects his or her divine beings to worship. Usually, the supreme being is thought about to be a genderless energy source like The Force in the Star Wars trilogy. This force is described as the All, and it consists of several elements of deep space. These aspects are shown in the manly and feminine energies of nature, which are shown in the form of different gods and goddesses existing in the world.

Individuals getting interested in Wicca mostly question just who or what the Pagan gods are. Are the images of the human mind developed by our forefathers? Are they stereotypical images of the cumulative human mind? Are they cosmic forces that antedate the human race? The response is not an easy one and should be discovered for oneself through training and experience.

This specific liberty to pursue and contemplate that which originates from within is what makes Witchcraft such an exceptional experience. There is no pressure to embrace another individual's concept or principle of divine being. There is no one, true, best, and only way. Everyone is considered to be accountable for his/her spiritual development, advancement, and relationship with deity.

The God

Like all divine beings, God has many faces. He looks like the radiant, fantastic, and illuminating Sun of Righteousness. To all those who indulge in the practice of Wicca, God exists as a sign of potency, the fertilizing, and regrowing force of nature. He personifies all that is masculine, powerful, and powerful.

The god's most apparent and dominant characteristic is his capability to regrow. His countenance might change with time and culture; he continually returns to live and die for the land he enjoys. He has been known as Osiris, Tammuz, and Adonis. He has manifested as the unconquered Sun or compassionate rescuer Mithra and Helios. Whatever his version, he is continuing the potentate of strength, authority, and power- and the final judgment before the eviction of the Goddess.

The Sun Cod

In Wicca, the existence of the divine is viewed in all the different aspects of nature. One of the most appreciated natural phenomena is that of the sun. This radiant ball of fire offers light, produces life, and promotes recovery. In addition to its timekeeping qualities, a crucial aspect of life, it has long represented God.

The Sun God was believed to rule the sky, and all that moved below it during the daytime. He presided over time, war, fertility, agriculture, and the regeneration of life. In the Romano-Celtic stage of Old Europe, the sun god was seen as being in a continuous fight with the forces of evil and darkness. To support the Sun God in the struggle against the powers of darkness, people worshiped him throughout morning routines. It was thought that these routines would provide him strength and help revive his brilliance each day.

The Harvest God

The god of greenery administered over the farming community as the child and lover of the great Mother Earth. He was highly personified in the Middle East as Tammuz, in Egypt as Osiris, and throughout ancient Europe as Dionysus and Adonis.

In ancient myths, the returning and passing away god, as portrayed in harvest rites, offered a way of redemption. To end up being part of his mystery custom was to guarantee for oneself a location within the structure of the afterlife.

To a lot of our ancestors, the harvest was a time of both event and mourning. The abundance of grain and white wine were cause for excellent delight.

The ancient misconceptions of Tammuz and Ishtar, Aphrodite and Adonis, and Isis and Osiris, best communicate this compelling drama of return, death, and life - all products of the harvest process. This cycle of growing, dying, and returning was the structure of the Pagan secrets that precede Christianity. It is also the main focus of most modern Wiccan customs.

When dealing with Wiccan gods, remember the main characteristics: The Sun God represents beauty, youth, and knowledge.

The Goddess

After centuries of exile, the goddess has made her way back to her land, people, and position as the personification of womanly perception and dominion. She is the Mistress of Magic; she is all that is charm and bounty. What the God inaugurates, the Goddess understands.

The Goddess is the instinctive and intuitive side of nature. Her incredible powers of shift and transformation radiate o

+like bright beams of celestial light, for she is the mystery and magic. Below her full, round moon she has been, and still is, conjured up as Arianrhod, Diana, and Hecate by those seeking her favors.

The Moon Goddess.

The moonlit the way for early human beings. The moon glowed in the night sky. Its light helped in guiding tourists, warriors, and hunters securely through the dark and back to their tribes.

As our ancestors sought to the heavens, they saw how the moon waxed and subsided, how the night was turned into day, spring into summer, and summer season into the winter season. They saw the seas ups and downs, plants come up with grain, and life burst forth from the womb. The Great Goddess highly worshiped in Old Europe became corresponded with the moon, in whose great light she was reflected. As the moon subsided and waxed, so did the Goddess' significant power and authority.

When the moon reached its full, pregnant magnificence, it was viewed as the Mother. Here we discover the nurturer, the provider of life and bringer of death, the Goddess's most potent, and indeed most revered stage. This was the time of excellent fertility and increased psychic awareness. It was a time typically set aside to visualize and formulate physical desires.

The subsiding moon saw the decrease of light and was connected with the Crone, who signified the manifestation process and was combined with knowledge. What was developed on the complete moon was realized during the waning moon. This was also a time of consideration and awareness of personal achievements.

As soon as the moon completes its three significant stages, it passes into a period of transition, referred to as the New Moon. This 3-day duration was and still is, considered the time of the Enchantress or Temptress-a time of terrific mystery and magic.

The Mother Goddess.

The Mother Goddess is a highly complicated figure, also the most influential figures within the Wiccan religion. She is the embodiment of feminine appeal, fertility, and the ability to support. In the old Pagan times, the Mother Goddess ruled over the fecundity of people and animals.

To our Pagan ancestors, the Mother Goddess enjoyed both was and feared. She was the tranquil benefactor in charge of regrowth, life, and fertility. As the Great Mother, she came up with experience, and as the Terrible Mother, she ruled over death and destruction.

Throughout ancient Europe, the Mother Goddess embraced a vast array of activities. Besides her association with fertility, she was likewise the embodiment of maturity and abundance. To portray these qualities, images of the Mother Goddess were endowed with large breasts, inflamed bellies, and full butts.

The principle of nurturing, with its ability to transcend the harsh realities of life and express genuine love, brings lots of people to the Goddess of Wicca. Their connection to the potential of the symptom process is reawakened once they are embraced by the Mother Goddess. When this takes place, people become able to get in touch with their nurturing potential, which develops spiritual maturity.

Picked Wiccan Goddesses.

Brigid: Celtic Triple Goddess. She is the embodiment of poetry, prophecy, and motivation. Brigid has initially been a fire, and the sun goddess understood as Brigid of the Golden Hair. Since her connection with the shooting, Brigid was associated with motivation and the art of smithcraft. Brigid was also a crucial fertility goddess. She was called on throughout birth to protect the mom and the child. Brigid's signs include the spindle, flame, well, ewe/lamb, snake, bell, and milk.

Cerridwen: Cerridwen, which is associated with Astarte or Demeter, is referred to as the mother goddess of the moon and grain. She is specifically known for her fearsome death totem, a white, corpse-eating plant. Cerridwen' s harvest events express her ability to both take and provide away life. Her symbols consist of the cup, sow, cauldron, and hound.

Diana (The Roman Moon Goddess): She was the patroness of hunters and guardians of the forest where her spiritual grove existed near Aricia. Diana's signs consist of the weapon, shoes, beautiful weapons, the dog, and the stag.

Demeter: Greek Earth Mother. As the goddess of vegetation, she was the creator of agriculture and the civic rite of marital relationships.

Isis (The Egyptian Mother Goddess): Isis is the personification of the Great Goddess in her aspect of maternal devotion. Isis was probably the biggest goddess in Egypt and was worshiped for more than 3,000 years. Her impact was not confined to Egypt and infected Greece and the Roman Empire. Isis was the female concept of nature and, for that reason, a goddess of a thousand names. Isis's signs include the Thet (knot or buckle), scepter, cup, horns, girdle, mirror, and snake.

Rhea (The Cretan Mother Goddess): Her name probably means Earth, and she was typically portrayed as a huge, magnificent lady surrounded by animals and small, subservient human males. Rhea was included in the Greek myth as a Titan, one of the second generation of deities. She was regarded as the goddess of the living earth. Rhea's symbols include the torch, double ax, brass drum, and trees bearing fruit.

The Morrigan (The Celtic Triple Goddess): The Morrigan is the dreadful hag goddess of the Celtic legend. She bears some relationship to the Furies and Valkyries of Norse Myth. She looks like a triple goddess of battle and illustrates the extreme, unrelenting warrior side of the Celtic soul. The Morrigan's s signs include the raven, crow, fight spear, shield, and ax.

When dealing with Wiccan goddesses, keep in mind primary attributes: Moon Goddess represents spiritual illumination and is the essence of magic and secret; Mother Goddess represents the sensual/nurturing side of the womanly nature and is filled with grace; and Triple Goddess exemplifies knowledge, seductiveness, and enchantment.

Seasons of the God and Goddess.

Wicca, like all mystery traditions, relies significantly on symbolism. When an individual sees a symbol, his or her consciousness is automatically elevated to a world of higher understanding. Religious art, objects, and charts are used to develop a bridge between the conscious and unconscious minds. They both expose and veil particular truths and facts according to each person's level of understanding.

The Seasons of the God and Goddess chart, which follows, is an excellent example of symbolic illustration. Taking a look at the table, one instantly grasps the relationship between time and divine being. Whereas the Goddess keeps a controlled and restrained position within the seasonal cycle, the God is more independent, less confined, and not as directly included with cyclic modification. It is typically accepted that feminine energy is more influential and involved with the cycles of nature than masculine energy is, even though the latter does have a dominating impact.

What is Witchcraft?

Those who identify as Wiccans and those who are Witches have differences of viewpoint relating to the term "Witchcraft." While not every Witchcraft is considered to be "Wiccan," the words "Wicca" and "Witchcraft" are frequently used interchangeably.

Some Wiccans argue for a difference between what they consider to be spirituality-based worship ("Wicca") and more "secular" practice (" Witchcraft"), however, mostly, the two are intertwined enough that the difference isn't especially beneficial.

With due regard to Wiccans who recognize a distinction, the term "Witchcraft" will be used in this book to explain the necessary activities found in rituals practiced by Wiccans and non-Wiccan Witches alike. Because some Wiccans do not practice magic and do not consider themselves Witches, the term "Witch" in this section of the book is used to refer those who both adopt Wiccan practices in some kind or another and practice magic as part of their religion.

Witchcraft is the set of practices and beliefs used by Witches in ritual and spellwork. Often, beautiful work is added to the Sabbat and Esbat events observed by covens and solitary Witches, though spell might be used by itself on other occasions. In reality, many Witches consider themselves to be continuously "practicing" their Craft in their every day lives through using meditation, amazingly charged meals and drinks, color choices in clothing and jewelry, nighttime candle routines, and other apparently "small" enactments of magic. The more one is in tune with the rhythms and energies of the natural world, the more "wonderful" one's life will feel and seem, and this relationship with the cycles of life is deepened throughout one's life through study and practice.

"Magic" is a word used for the phenomena that happen when people knowingly take part in the co-creative forces of the Universe, by using the subtle energies of nature to trigger the necessary change in their truth.

People may use magic, or "the Craft" as it is frequently called, for many purposes. This often includes spells, appeals, and other operations for what could be called "personal gain," such as a new job or improvements in a love relationship. However, the Craft is also used to work for benefits to one's household, neighborhood, and even to individuals around the world. A coven might use an Esbat ritual as a chance to send out beneficial recovery light to victims of a natural disaster. What the Craft is not used for is anything that would cause harm to another person or other living beings, even unintentionally. Our dreams can often be manipulative when it concerns how they impact other individuals, even when we do not understand it. For that reason, routine and spellwork frequently consist of safeguards versus unintentional abuse of magical energy, such as the phrases "for the good of all" and "harm to none"-- taken from the Wiccan Rede. Keeping this idea in the leading edge of one's mind is essential, especially in light of another basic tenet of Witchcraft: the Threefold Law.

The Threefold Law

Also called "The Rule of Three" and "The Law of Return," this principle specifies that everything witches send out into the Universe as intent, whether negative or positive, will come back to them three times as fantastic. While some Witches don't go with this particular belief, it is usually conjured up as a suggestion that incredible power should be used just for good, and never in the spirit of damage or manipulation.

Magic and Science

Many modern authors on Witchcraft have explained the relevance of discoveries in the physical sciences that seem to determine what Witches have always known to exist: a cooperative relationship between mind and matter.

This relationship can be viewed from numerous angles and is probably not entirely understood by anybody. Still, its presence is glaring to professionals of magic as well as other mind/thought-based disciplines that cause favorable modification in one's life.

The standard worldview of the majority of Western society for the past couple of centuries has held that truth is chaotic and inflexible, developed by forces beyond human control. It has likewise held that the mind is not a physical entity, and is separate from what we believe of as "matter." What Witches understand, and what science has begun to discover, is that reality is versatile, and is co-created by and with everything in it, consisting of the mind.

The power of an idea has been brightened in many books and videos about the "Law of Attraction," a "New Age" subject that has just recently found popularity among mainstream audiences, celebrities, and even company professionals. The Law mentions that ideas draw in experiences that reinforce them, so that home on negative situations can keep them in place, while concentrating on favorable experiences produces improved circumstances. Altering one's thoughts is more complicated than it may appear, of course, which is perhaps why a lot of information and advice regarding the Law of Attraction is currently readily available.

The Hermetic Principles

Witchcraft can be stated to employ the Law of attraction in a sense, though magic can be much more intricate than just focusing one's ideas on a preferred outcome. It might be more accurate to state that Witches use routines, tools, words, and presents from the natural world to improve and broaden their deal with the Hermetic Principles.

The Hermetic Principles date back to late antiquity and have notified Western religious, philosophical, esoteric, and clinical ideas. They have intriguing parallels in modern physics, consisting of quantum mechanics and string theory, and explain the method reality operates on a subatomic level, where all product things are composed of energy and radiate energy. Lots of Witches have been watching excitedly as the scientific understanding of the makeup of deep space unfolds to validate what ancient observers understood.

There are seven Hermetic Principles, which are typically referred to in most discussions of magic. One of the most emphasized is the Law of Correspondence, which mentions that what is correct on the macrocosm is likewise real on the microcosm. This suggests that every particle of matter contains all others-- and that linear time on the physical aircraft represents just one dimension in the ultimately spaceless and classic overall Universe. Another way of stating the concept is "as above, so below, as listed below, so above." The more enormous planes of existence influence the lower planes of presence, and vice versa. As microcosms of the Universe, we can glean info from the far-off past, view pictures of the future through divination, and alter our reality.

A widely-reported and recent research study discovered that the laws governing the development of the Universe share substantial resemblances to the development of both the human brain and the Internet.

Just as every particle of matter consists of all others, matter and energy all include info at their the majority of basic level. The Universe, eventually, is mental at its highest level, which is the underlying innovative force of all things. We understand that all the developments, developments, and adjustments in our human history started as concepts. Witches also understand that ideas can affect the Universal mind, and this is part of why focused intent in ritual is essential.

The Law of Vibration holds that whatever remains in continuous movement, and that absolutely nothing is at rest. This applies even to relatively sturdy physical things such as tables and chairs-- they have vibrations than we just can't view with the human mind-matter is comprised of energy, which is essentially a force moving at a specific wave. The parallel with animism deserves noting here, as animists believe that whatever is alive. If a quality of being "alive" is to be in motion, then the animists have been appropriate the whole time.

The nature of colors as light moving at various rates of vibration is particularly helpful in Witchcraft, as each color's frequency has particular attributes ideal for specific purposes. We frequently associate love with the colors red and pink, for instance, and it ends up that these colors resonate with energies in the body that promote loving sensations. Therefore, these colors, when used in spellwork to bring love into one's life, both communicate that information appropriately to the Universe and connect it to the Witch's energy field. Naturally, like all things, colors can have their disadvantages. The high vibration of the color red can also overstimulate and activate unpleasant feelings. Color treatments utilizing the Chakra system and meditation techniques often seek to stabilize out-of-whack fluctuations in the body, and colors can

Be used amazingly in much the same method.

Comprehending systems like the Hermetic Principles and the Law of Attraction can be useful in increasing one's success in magic. However, a thorough grounding in them is not completely necessary. And it's valuable to remember that no matter how effective the intentions for magic might be, outcomes may be restricted by the unknown universal truths of the real and more magnificent airplanes-- sometimes we're just not implied to get precisely what we want at a particular time. It may be that somebody else would be hurt in some way, or that something else is already around the corner that will look after our needs differently.

Witches can learn a lot about the nature of deep space by observing which of their unusual operations be successful, and which do not. The study of the Craft is thought about by most to be a long-lasting pursuit, with ongoing learning and refining of practices. When thinking about the relationship between the growth of the Universe and the development of the human brain, the wisdom of continuous study makes even more sense. As more knowing occurs, more magical techniques are developed and established, and there's all the more to capture upon.

Routine and Spellwork

It may be said that Wicca, as a religion, recognizes the laws of the Universe symbolically through the Goddess and God, the Wheel of the Year, and reverence for all living things.

Routines performed in celebration of these elements of deep space might or might not involve fantastic work, as some Wiccans prefer to

focus on what they see as the "spiritual" side of life. Witches, on the other hand, tend to blend routine with magic, and may focus solely on working to transform reality for the benefit of themselves and others. This does not always imply they don't consider themselves spiritual. If all matter includes all matter, then there is no separation between mental issues and the issues of everyday life.

Whether magic is being worked in a provided routine, Wiccans and other Witches tend to integrate a couple of common structures in their official activities, including casting a magical or sacred circle, conjuring up deities and special powers using unique words and phrases, and closing the loop at the end of the ritual. Motion, dance, shouting, or singing might likewise be part of the activities.

These formal actions communicate to the higher realms of deep space the thoughts and intents of the specialist(s) in a focused and productive manner, concentrating the energies of objective clearly and definitively. Voltage, as physical matter, is raised in ritual and directed towards specific purposes, whether for thankfulness and event, manifesting solutions to problems, or both.

Casting the Circle

As a symbol, the circle represents the Moon, the Earth, and the abundance of the Goddess. For this reason, a ring can safely contain the physical quantity of energy raised by the Witch or Witches carrying out the ritual, and see its transformation through to the higher realms. The circle is a considerably portable tool, as it can be drawn anywhere, either physically or psychically, subtly or elaborately, depending upon the scenarios.

The circle is small or as massive as suitable. However, it needs to have enough space for the altar, everything being used in the routine, and everybody getting involved-- I'll be introducing to you the platform and ritual tools in the next area. It is generally marked on the floor of the area being utilized for ritual, often with sea salt first, followed by candles, or other magical items charged with energy for ceremonies, such as crystals and semiprecious gemstones, and even herbs.

When energy is raised inside the circle, the circle should remain closed until the end of the ritual. This keeps the heat from joining distracting or unsuitable power from the rest of the real airplane, which reinforces the magic and protects professionals from unwanted energetic interference.

Nobody can step beyond the circle while it is active without first carrying out an energetic manipulation, such as a "circle-cutting" spell, which creates a dynamic "doorway" that is safe to reenter and exit. When the circle is re-entered, the door is closed, and the circle reconnected.

Calling the Quarters

Referred to as "drawing the quarters," this is a method of acknowledging the four primary directions and their Elemental associations, as well as the chosen divine beings of the coven or solitary Witch.

In a coven, either the High Priestess, the High Priest, or another coven member will walk the circle, stopping in each cardinal instructions to invoke the existence of its associated Element and, if suitable, god or goddess. (It must be remembered here that not all coven structures involve hierarchy-- some covens just have each member take turns performing this and any other necessary roles in ritual.) Specific words are typically spoken to invoke the special powers and true blessings of the component and deity being called. Once this is complete, the space is prepared for the heart of the routine.

Types of Ritual

The heart of the ritual may be a Sabbat or Esbat event, or it may celebrate a life occasion such as an initiation into a coven, a self-introduction for eclectic and singular Witches, a handfasting (wedding), or an end of life ceremony. There are as many variations on each of these types of routine as there are covens and solitary professionals, and the way a specific Sabbat or Esbat is commemorated may alter and change throughout the years. In truth, many routines are made up on the spot.

Moreover, the majority of covens don't share information about their rituals with non-members. All of this makes it challenging to generalize about the proceedings of routine in Witchcraft. Lots of examples are available in books about the Craft and on Other and Wiccan Pagan websites.

At some point during the ritual, fantastic spells may be worked. Prophecy may also be employed, particularly at Samhain, though this may take location after the ceremony. When all of the ritual work is finished, the circle is closed, frequently in an opposite way to the way it is opened, with the Witch thanking and dismissing the Elements and divine beings conjured up at the start, while strolling in the opposite instructions. This guarantees that the energy raised during ritual has gone entirely to its destination in the higher worlds, and is not squandered or ignored in the physical plane. It likewise assists ground the Witch(es) more firmly in the real airplane after reaching extreme states of awareness.

Magical Work

The types, forms, and intentions of fantastic work occurring during a Wiccan ritual are as differed as every other aspect of Wicca and Witchcraft: It may include any mix of actions, tools, words, complicated or easy spellwork, a tea or brew, chanting and motion, candlelight work, etc

. The choices for magical discovery are genuinely limitless. The function of the magic can also be anything under the sun-- as long as the effect is positive, and does no damage. Numerous Wiccans pick to work for spiritual in addition to material development, utilizing the Sabbats as opportunities to review their lives at each point in the Wheel and work for balance or any necessary change.

However, magical work does not need to become part of the Wiccan routine, and isn't limited to it. Witches will include incredible job, as they are likely and able to do so, into any part of their lives.

The tools described in the next area are utilized in both Wiccan routine and lots of other forms of Witchcraft, in the ways and for the functions that feel suitable to the Witch(es) who utilize them.

The Tools

Wiccans, as well as other Witches, incorporate a variety of items into their routines and magic, a number of which are familiar to traditional culture

-- you may have become aware of a few of these tools, and even have the ability to picture what they appear like, from viewing television and movies.

However, their discussion in the movie theater is frequently incorrect, with more emphasis put on entertainment rather than being depicting the reality of a tool's usage and purpose. For this reason, much of the Wiccan tools are misunderstood.

Given that the Universe is made of the idea, it is eventually the thought energy behind the actions performed with the tools that cause improvement of truth.

- **Broom**

Perhaps the most typical (and commonly misunderstood) sign of Witches and Witchcraft in popular culture, the broom has become part of Wiccan and other pagan lore around the world for centuries. The spiritual brush is not always used in the official Wiccan routine itself; however, it is typically utilized to sweep energetic clutter from the ritual area in advance. The bristles do not, in fact, have to touch the ground, as this sort of cleansing is taking place on the energetic and psychic level.

Because it functions as a cleanser, it is associated with the component of Water, and is spiritual to the Goddess. The broom can also be positioned near the entrance to a house to protect versus unfavorable or undesirable energy.

The broom can be any size, from miniature "decorative" brooms to bigger, full-sized brushes. It might even be a tree-branch utilized symbolically as a broom. Standard woods used for sacred brooms include birch, ash, and willow. Lots of Witches keep hand-made brushes for ritual functions. However, a typical home broom can also be devoted to the work of Witchcraft. No matter what type of product, nevertheless, the regular brush is never utilized for everyday housekeeping, as this would contaminate the sacred energy it holds for routine and magical purposes.

- **Altar**

The altar is the sacred location where tools are positioned during Wiccan ritual and magic. Generally, the platform stands in the center of the circle of energy raised by the participant(s) in the ceremony. It might be a table or other item with a flat surface, such as an old chest. It can be square or round, according to choice. Witches may embellish the altar with colored scarves or other products corresponding with the season or the particular function of the routine.

Ideally, the altar is made of wood, such as oak, which is considered to hold significant power, or willow, which is deemed to be spiritual to the goddess. It can actually be made of any product, as any real things charged with magical energy will contribute power to the routine work being enacted.

Witches performing outside routines might utilize an old tree stump, large stone, or other natural item for an altar, or may use a fire in place of the altar, putting the routine tools in other places in the charged space.

While the altar is usually set up prior to the ritual and taken down later, some Witches preserve long-term altars in their homes. These may function as shrines to the Goddess and God, and can be a place to keep the Witch's wonderful tools.

The tools are strategically positioned in specific styles on the altar, with deliberate regard to the components and the four instructions. For instance, tools and symbols related to the element of Earth may be placed in the North area of the altar, while those connected with water will be put to the East. Traditional Wiccan practice also typically devotes the left side of the altar to representations of the Goddess, while the ideal team represents the God. While numerous Witches carefully follow established patterns for setting up the platform, others will experiment and use designs that resonate with their relationship with their deities and matching tools and symbols.

- **Wand**

Used for millennia in magical and spiritual rites, the wand has long been connected with Witches and Witchcraft in popular culture, and has likewise been wholly misunderstood.

Similar to all wonderful tools, it is not the wand that causes magical transformation; however, the Witch, who energetically charges the rod with high intent. As a shape, it takes the type of a line; therefore, it is used to direct energy. It is typically used in Wiccan routine to conjure up the Goddess and God, and maybe utilized to draw magical signs in the air or on the ground. It may also be effectively used to illustrate the circle within which the ritual or spellwork is carried out. The wand is connected with the aspect of Air, and is considered spiritual to the God.

The wand can be a relatively straightforward affair, simply cut from a small branch or twig from a tree (with a mindset of respect and regard for the tree making the sacrifice). Generally, the wand isn't much longer than the forearm, and can be much shorter. Woods traditionally utilized to make the rod include oak, willow, senior, and hazel. Witches without access to these or other trees might buy a wood dowel from a craft or hardware shop to consecrate and embellish as a wand. There are also some exquisite glass or pewter-based rods embellished with engravings and crystals readily available at lots of New Age shops. Still, wood is the traditional product for Wiccan wands, and it is typically thought that a rod made by the Witch who uses it is more effective.

- **Knife**

Called an athame, the ritual knife, like the wand, is a tool that directs energy in ritual, and may likewise be utilized to draw the circle before ritual and close the loop afterward.

Nevertheless, it is more of an energy manipulator or commander, due to its sharp edges, and therefore isn't commonly used to invoke divine beings, as this would be considered robust, instead of collective, in regards to working with high energy. The athame is also utilized to draw beautiful symbols, such as the pentagram, in the air to lend power to routine and spellwork, and is frequently employed in methods that eradicate and launch negative energies or impacts. This tool is related to the God, and the component of Fire, as it is a representative that triggers modification.

The knife is typically sharp on both sides, with a black deal with which is stated to save a percentage of the radiant energy raised in routines for later use. The blade is not typically really long-- the length of one's hand, or shorter, is thought about perfect.

Some Witches purchase special daggers to serve as their athame, while others will consecrate a regular cooking area knife for the purpose. It's thought about unwise to utilize a knife that has been used to cut animal flesh. However, any negative energies lingering from such usage can be ritually cleaned before "transforming" the blade into an athame. Some Witches choose to enhance their energetic relationship with their knife by inscribing excellent symbols into the deal with.

Depending on the custom, the athame may do double duty as a real cutting and engraving tool. It may be used to cut herbs, shape a brand-new wand from the branch of a tree, or carve magical symbols into a candle for routine usage. Nevertheless, many Witches prefer to use a second, white-handled knife (often called a boline) for these functions, keeping the athame for ritual usage just.

- **Cauldron**

While the word "cauldron" may evoke images of Shakespeare's three witches tossing all sorts of animal parts into a boiling stew for wicked functions, the cauldron is a sign of the Goddess and the innovative forces of change. Containers appear in several ancient Celtic myths in connection with magical incidents, and continue to influence Witchcraft today. Related to the aspect of Water, the cauldron might hold amazingly charged active ingredients for a potion, or might be utilized to permit spell candle lights to stress out. It can likewise be filled with freshwater and used for scrying.

Cast iron is considered the cauldron's perfect product, though other metals are typically used. A lot of rest on three legs, with the opening of the cauldron having a smaller diameter than the best part of the bowl. Cauldrons can vary from a few inches to a couple of feet across in size, though bigger sizes may be thought about not practical. While some Witches might brew an excellent potion right in the cauldron, the reasonable restraints of lighting a safe indoor fire below it tend to limit this use-- often, the "brewing" aspect of the magic is symbolic rather than actual.

- **Cup**

Like the cauldron, the cup represents the aspect of Water and represents the fertility of the Goddess.

A crucial element of the altar layout during a routine, it might hold water, white wine, or potentially a unique tea brewed for the wonderful purpose of the rite. In some routines, it stays empty, as a symbol of preparedness to receive new sources of abundance from the Spirit world. Likewisecalled the "goblet" or the "chalice" in some traditions, it can be made of any quality compound such as earthenware, crystal, glass, or silver. Singular Witches may simply commit a favorite old household cup, charging it with magical energy and keeping it simple for this function.

- **Pentacle**

The pentacle is an important symbol-bearer in Witchcraft, usually inscribed with a pentagram, though other wonderful symbols might be available. The pentagram itself is a five-pointed star, drawn with five straight lines, typically encircled, and constantly having one upward point. Each point is said to represent the aspects of Air, Earth, Fire, and Water, with the Fifth Element (Spirit) as the upward point.

As a sign, it is discovered in both ancient Eastern and Western cultures and has been used to represent numerous elements of spiritual and human concerns. The pentagram is considered to have intrinsic magical powers, and is often inscribed on items in addition to in the air throughout rituals, to include strength to the work.

As a bearer of this Earth-related symbol, the pentacle is utilized to consecrate other tools and objects used in ritual. Typically a flat, round piece of wood, silver, wax, or clay, it can be any size, though typically is small enough to fit conveniently on the altar with the other tools. The pentacle might be ornately carved and set with semiprecious gemstones, or maybe an effortless style. Witches may also use a pentacle on a cable or chain throughout the ritual, and even as part of their daily gown, though they might or might pass by to wear it publicly.

• **Incense**

Incense is associated with the aspect of Air, and, in some customs, Fire. Smoldering incense is often positioned before images of the deities on an altar or a shrine. Many Witches feel that fragrance is a vital component of effective ritual. This is partly due to the consciousness-altering potential of quality incense, which can help with a more concentrated state of mind when performing magical work.

Smoke from the incense can likewise offer visions of the deities being conjured up in routine, or other images essential to the work being carried out. Particular herbs, spices, barks, and roots have specific magical qualities, so homemade incense blends can be utilized to strengthen magical spells.

Whether homemade or store-bought, regular Wiccan routines prefer granulated or raw incense, which needs charcoal briquettes to burn on, and is usually held in a censer. Some

Witches may let the scent smolder in the cauldron instead of a censer.

For Witches who are more sensitive to incense smoke, lighter stick or cone incenses may work better. Some go with scenting their magical candles with oils rather. Whatever the choice, it's typically agreed that some form of fragrant enhancement is optimal for magical work.

- **Crystals, Stones, Herbs, and Oils**

Possibly a few of the most effective magical tools are those that come straight from the Earth without much, if any, modification by human hands. Herbs and semiprecious gems have long been understood to have healing homes, and are used today in lots of medical systems around the globe. They are likewise utilized in Witchcraft, as decors, offerings, magical improvements, and even as the focus of some routines and spells.

Crystals and other stones have their energies and are considered to be "alive," instead of just dormant matter. Sensitive people can frequently feel their energies when holding these stones in their hands or on some other part of their bodies.

Some stones are used for specific functions in routine, while others might be more irreversible existences on the altar or in other places in a Witch's home. They might range in size from a square half-inch to much more significant, and maybe polished and sculpted into specific shapes, or left in their raw type. Crystals can be found in many New Age stores along with online, though they can, in some cases, still be found in their raw form in specific natural areas.

Crystals might be utilized to help defend against illness or negative energy, or may aid in divination or other psychic work. They might also be used to layout the magic circle at the start of the routine. These stones have astrological associations as well as associations with specific gods and goddesses.

Herbs are likewise associated with astrological bodies and specific deities, and are utilized in a variety of ways, consisting of excellent cooking area brews, edibles, and potions, and spell active ingredients. A few of the most common kitchen herbs, such as basil, thyme, and rosemary, also have magical associations, which doubles their capacity for practical magic, as they can be used to make "enchanted" foods.

Other herbs utilized in magic are not suitable to consume, and care needs always to be taken to understand the difference. It is considered ideal for Witches to collect their herbs with their routine knives, whether from a nearby woods or their own kitchen herb "gardens." However, fresh herbs can be discovered in grocery shops, and numerous natural food shops also sell a variety of dried herbs in their bulk departments.

Essential oils from nuts, seeds, and plants are used to boost routine environment and likewise as components in spellwork. Oils have esoteric properties and might be rubbed into spell candle lights for a particular excellent purpose, or used in a skin-safe blend to anoint the

body prior to the ritual. Witches often make their own blends of vital oils to strengthen routine and spellwork. Also used in aromatherapy for recovery a number of psychological and physical ailments, essential oils are commonly offered at health food stores.

- **Candle lights**

Last, however, certainly not least, candles are thought-about necessary to the practice of Witchcraft.

Candle lights have a magical way about them as they permit us to work straight with the component of fire. They serve as a source of light, as devotional signs of deity, as a way of communicating with Spirit, and to help change in many spells.

Witches deal with a range of candle light colors, depending on the deities being represented and/or invoked, in addition to any particular wonderful purposes of a routine or spell. Candles are a direct and basic way to deal with color magic. Colors have their own metaphysical properties, as well as astrological and elemental associations, which will be described in the next area of this guide.

Witches will usually identify in between candle lights used for particular routine functions and more "multi-purpose" candle lights utilized for additional lighting throughout spellwork (or merely to enhance any night atmosphere). Candle lights consecrated for wonderful use are therefore not used for any other purposes.

Other Tools

Depending upon the custom, the coven, and the specific Witch, additions and variations to the tools described above may be utilized in ritual and spellwork. For example, some Witches utilize a sword in addition to, or in a location of, the routine knife. Swords can be not practical for indoor routine due to their size, and are not as easily accessible as knives, and so are less typically utilized.

A staff is likewise often used in formal routine, held by the High Priest or Priestess of a coven. Like the wand, it brings the representations of Air and the God, though, in some customs, it represents Fire. It is typically made of wood and might be decorated with wonderful signs and semiprecious stones.

Lots of Witches also incorporate prophecy tools in their ritual practice. These may consist of runes, tarot cards, a quartz crystal sphere (or "crystal ball") for scrying or other oracles borrowed from older customs, such as the I-Ching. Specific items, such as a particular Tarot card or rune, might be included in spells for particular purposes. The crystal sphere is typically utilized on the altar to represent the Goddess. As mentioned previously, divination might occur during an official routine, however, post-ritual is likewise considered an excellent time for this activity, as the Witch is still in a conducive state of mind to communicate with the Spirit world at this time.

Lastly, lots of Witches like to consist of amazingly charged jewelry and other aspects of "outfit" into their practice. Some may simply wear a pentacle on a chain, as pointed out above, while others may put on unique robes and a headpiece encrusted with gemstones to enhance their energy throughout the ritual. Witches in some customs likewise work naked, which is typically referred to as "sky-clad.".

Just like any other element of Wicca and Witchcraft, there is no set-in-stone way to approach utilizing the tools of routine and magic. While it's generally considered handy to use at least a couple of, if not numerous, of the mechanisms described above, it is ultimately about the Witch and his or her connection to the specific tools selected, or the coven members' cumulative affinities for the specifics of their ritual practice. Those recognizing as Wiccans are likely to have some symbolic representation of the Goddess and God at Sabbat celebrations, and the Goddess at Esbats, but the method this is performed can differ extensively.

While some solitaries and covens may develop intricate routines utilizing every tool imaginable, others may develop extremely basic affairs, including just a crystal and candlelight. In other words, it's more about using what feels inspiring and "in tune," rather than collecting items from a checklist-- if it feels out of location, or unpleasantly unusual to a particular Witch to buy and utilize a cauldron or a censer, or wear unique robes, then these items might simply not be essential or suitable for that person.

This is, naturally, a really brief introduction of the basic concepts, tools, and forms associated with Wicca and other Witchcraft, as opposed to a thorough conversation-- as is to be expected with such a different and commonly varying faith as Wicca, other sources will have different things to say about a number of the subjects talked about here. Readers interested in discovering more ought to seek advice from as many referrals as they please for a much deeper understanding of these beliefs and practices.

For those considering adopting any or all of the practices talked about in this guide, the next area will explore numerous practical steps one can take on their journey towards practicing Wicca.

CHAPTER THIRTEEN

Tips For Aspiring Wiccans

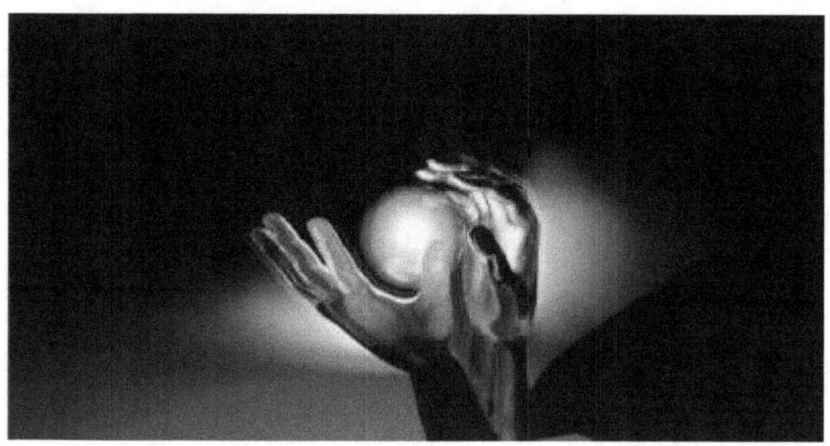

- **Moving Forward**

Wicca is different from other religious beliefs in many aspects. It doesn't tend to be evangelistic or look for new members; you won't discover numerous fliers welcoming you to the next Sabbat celebration with your local coven.

This leaves it to the individuals intrigued in the Craft to look for info and possible connections with others in the Wiccan community. Luckily, the Internet has made it far much more comfortable than it used to be for Witches and Wiccans to post and find info and interact with each other.

- **Read And Check Out**

The very best way to start is to read widely about Wicca and other kinds of Paganism. If you read commonly enough, you'll come across conflicting beliefs and recommendations, and this is an excellent thing, as it enables you to establish your understanding of the forces and phenomena at work in Wicca and Witchcraft. Follow what resonates with you at the deepest level. If a ritual, spell, any other idea, or a particular viewpoint does not attract you, leave it out of your establishing practice and keep seeking more information that feels "ideal." A lot of Wiccans and Witches will inform you that it takes a long period to study and observe to produce an authentic individual relationship with the Craft.

If you're looking to link with others, depending upon where you live, there may be a local coven, circle, or other such groups that you could join or find a way out for information and recommendations. You can likewise examine event listings online, in regional newspapers, or other neighborhood resources. You can send out an intent to the Universe to assist in bringing the people you're looking for into your life, and it may be that a group near you is looking for somebody new to sign up with and will look forward to receiving your message!

You can also always begin your own "study group" to discover like-minded souls who also wish to find out more about Wicca, Witchcraft, or other forms of Paganism.

- **Coven, Circle, Solitary, Or Eclectic?**

For people interested in working with other Wiccans and Covens, circles and witches can be a great way to get more robust training and advice from experienced practitioners. The terms "coven" and "circle" can be confusing for newbies, as they typically appear to be used interchangeably. They are not, nevertheless, the same thing.

A circle is generally a relatively informal group whose members may get together to find out and talk about the Craft and might try out the different types of routine and spellwork. They might or might not fulfill for Sabbats and Esbats, depending on the collective wishes of the group. Depending upon how "open" the group is, there might be numerous members, some of whom drop in and out as it matches them, or simply a few routinely included good friends. The structure of a circle is typically loose and does not need official initiation or involves an established hierarchy.

A coven, on the other hand, is more structured and typically has several established leaders, such as a High Priestess or High Priest, particularly in what is described as "Traditional" Wicca. Covens meet for Esbats and Sabbats, and members are anticipated to go to these gatherings, as the involvement of everyone is necessary to the routine. Initiation is usually needed, though it's somewhat not likely that somebody brand-new to Wicca will be rapidly initiated into a coven, for a few factors.

One is that covens are generally small groups, with seven being considered an ideal number, and there's a custom of not more than 13 members, if there's sufficient reason to push a coven past 13, one member will depart to start a new, separate coven. Depending on how well established a coven is, there might just merely not be any openings.

Secondly, coven members will want potential brand-new initiates to have spent a good deal of time studying before considering inviting them to take part in the official routine.

Finally, given that the bonds formed between coven members are relatively intimate and strong, the concern of whether somebody's personality and general energy are a good fit is an important one.

For those who do not live near any circles or covens, or who just prefer not to include a social aspect into their experience of the Craft, the life of a diverse or singular Witch can be simply as significant and fulfilling. Perhaps you 'd rather be familiar with the magical and spiritual dimensions of the Universe on your own for a while, and then consider connecting to like-minded others, or maybe you're just born to be a solo specialist, who's completely fine! No matter which instructions you pick, there's a myriad of scholarly sources out there to guide you along the way.

The terms "solitary" and "eclectic" may often be used interchangeably, as there can be a great deal of overlap, but the differences deserve explaining here. " Solitary" refers to the practice of Wicca or Witchcraft on one's own, without any group experience such as a coven or circle. Wiccans who come from covens may (and frequently do) still practice by themselves, along with their involvement in coven work. However, a Solitary Wiccan or Witch always works alone. A singular Witch can even intentionally follow what is typically accepted be "Traditional" Wicca, such as Gardnerian, British Traditional Wicca, or another "lineage-based" tradition, and those who do so tend to determine as "singular" rather than "diverse.".

" Eclectic" is a description for Witches who do not follow a single, particular tradition and instead borrow and blend concepts, techniques, practices, etc. from a range of sources, and might also (and typically do) invent their own. Some covens likewise consider themselves to be "eclectic," although this tends to irritate members of traditional covens.

It's worth remembering here that even the earliest recognized kinds of Traditional Wicca were primarily obtained, mixed, and " invented" themselves.

Finding Your Way In.

In this area, I want to show you how a newcomer to Wicca may begin to embrace the Wiccan beliefs, way of living, and rituals.

- **Living through the Wheel of the Year.**

Wicca and Witchcraft are rooted in a relationship with nature and its different expressions in plant and animal life, the aspects, and the turning of the seasons. The living, breathing Divine Mind is vibrantly present in nature, maybe more certainly so than in many of the human-made, modern-day, "industrialized world." Those interested in Wicca and Witchcraft will benefit from consciously observing the natural world around them and establishing a more deliberate relationship with it.

Witches who live in climates with four different seasons (Spring, Summer, Autumn, and Winter) have an exceptional opportunity to observe the Wheel of the Year carefully. Sabbats are the very best time to keep in mind the modifications on the Earth and in the sky over the last several weeks, and Esbats also provide celebrations for marking the seasons' effects in our everyday lives. The more you take note of the area "in-between seasons," the more the motion of the Earth ends up being obvious even in Winter.

If you live in an environment with less seasonal range, or even none at all to speak of, you can still observe the effects of natural forces in subtle methods. The sun still casts various qualities of light throughout the day. The air tends to change simply before the rain. Ending up being practiced in the practice of observing little details in your natural surroundings helps cultivate your openness to the hidden energies inherent in all of the Universe.

If you can, go out for walks, hikes, picnics, etc. in places with soil and vegetation. Or go swimming, canoeing, or rock-skipping throughout a pond. Construct a snowman or shape your creation in snow. Do whatever you can to invest some quality time outdoors regularly.

If you reside in an urban environment and have little in the way of access to natural areas, you can still produce ways to interact with the hidden forces of deep space. Parks can be ideal, however, so can indoor plants and windowsill gardens. You can grow herbs for magical use and recovery, along with cooking. Open a window at dawn and study whatever you can see of the sky. Stand in the rain for a minute and accept the sensation of it on your skin. Even nature programs and photos or art portraying natural scenes can help put you in touch, along with recordings of nature sounds and meditation music.

When Sabbats come around, make a point of gathering a few of the seasonal presents of the Earth-- flower petals in Spring months leaves shed from deciduous trees in Autumn, pine needles from evergreens in Winter. Use these in routine, or just as designs on your cooking area table or elsewhere where you'll see them typically. As you practice these ways of observing the Wheel of the Year, you'll find your relationship with the seasons (even your least preferred ones) becoming more attuned and rooted in appreciation.

- **Deities And The Divine.**

Seeking and attaining a spiritual relationship with the Triple Goddess or Cernunnos or Diana or any other number of divine beings from around the ancient world can be an extremely effective method into the Craft, and lots of people find their experience to be deepened and sharpened through the practice of more standard, structured types of Wicca.

Some beginners to Wicca and Witchcraft are not sure about the concept of "worshipping" deities, and may feel odd about browsing for one or more specific gods or goddesses to form relationships or alignments with. Loaning from older customs in this regard might not quite seem like an authentic method to a spiritual search.

It indeed takes time to discover and cultivate an interest in and a relationship with a deity you weren't familiar with until just recently, and individuals who were raised in monotheistic religious beliefs can have a hard time even more with integrating the idea of polytheism. It's likewise real that you don't have to incorporate a faith in or a relationship with any particular form of the divine. You may just deal with the concept of a Goddess and a God, and even less definitively recognized energies of the Universe.

Faith and belief are far more frequently established and cultivated gradually than right away achieved. Make an effort to study and seek yours, however, go at your rate, and trust your intuition. Because your relationship with the divine doesn't match their experience, no one can inform you you're not a real Wiccan or Witch. (Well, some might, however, in religion with numerous variations, it's just natural that some will quibble about the details.) There's no intermediary in between you and deep space, and there are as numerous paths to the Divine as there are individuals who seek it.

If you do see getting in touch with deities as a possible part of your path, begin doing some research study. Check them out in Wiccan books, in ancient misconceptions, in poetry, in history books. You may find, as some Witches do, that a deity will discover you through images, dreams, relatively "random" coincidences or events, or in other ways.

- **Meditation and Visualization.**

Getting ready for ritual and magical work includes accessing an advantageous altered state of mind that permits both openness and focus. Lots of traditions practice particular meditation and visualization techniques to enhance this ability and call on it when required. You can find information on meditation in Witchcraft or lots of other spiritual customs. Seek out various kinds of meditation instruction and practice what works best for you. If absolutely nothing else, be sure to set aside time and space for privacy and reflection, preferably every day, however absolutely before routine and spellwork.

A Ritual of Celebration and Magic Adopted for the Autumn Equinox.

This reasonably simple ritual is provided as one example of many possibilities-- I've included it to reveal you an example of one of the more accessible, and easy-to-perform routines for the novice Wiccan. It's created for solitary practice but could be adapted for use with a coven. Like the majority of routines, it can be tailored to your intuition, choices, or circumstances. (It can likewise be duplicated for other Sabbats, with modifications made to seasonal products, candle colors, etc.) You need to have a candle or two at least, and some kind of recognition of the season to serve as points of focus for your energy remember, most of the tools are symbolic as the power comes from you.

However, tools are especially useful for beginners as they provide them something tangible to focus and direct their energy onto.

Are you prepared to begin?

Given That the Autumn Equinox is a time for commemorating the abundance of the harvest, styles for focus in ritual consist of appreciation to the Sun for making the harvest possible and to the Earth for yielding plenty to finish the Winter months.

The balance of equivalent day and equivalent night is likewise excellent to observe, as is the opportunity to begin a turning inward and eagerly anticipating a more relaxing time. When the abundance of the Earth starts to die back to make room for brand-new development in the next cycle, the end of Summer is also a time. We can use this time to recognize what in our lives isn't required any longer, whether it be excessive "things," an old habit we've wished to break, or anything else that we 'd like to release back into deep space.

As you prepare for the routine, practice meditation on these styles and observe what comes to mind. See this opportunity to gain insight into an element of your life; you might not have been conscious of previously.

Advised items:

- Seasonal representations such as late summer season crops, mainly corn and squash, marigolds, seeds, and apples.
- Candle lights: 1 black, one white, one dark green spell candle, and one or more others in fall colors like red, orange, brown, gold, etc.
- Pentacle Cup Incense or oils: frankincense, sandalwood, pine, rosemary, chamomile Stones: jade, carnelian, lapis lazuli Herbs: sage, Hawthorne, cedar Instructions: Layout your tools on your altar or ritual space.

One way is to position the white candlelight on the left for the Goddess, the black candle on the right for the God, the pentacle to the North, and the cup to the West. Candlelight can be positioned in the South, this can be the spell of candlelight, if you're using it. Incense or oils can be put in the East. (If it's not useful to position burning incense right on the altar, you can position it somewhere close by in the Eastern quarter.) Any stones or representations of the harvest can be placed around the edges of the altar or wherever they seem to "want" to be. Take some time trying various arrangements. You'll soon get a sense of what feels and looks right for you.

If you wish to cast a circle, ensure you have everything you're using for the routine, and then decide how big your ring will require to be. Using sea salt, sprayed candle lights, stones, or herbs, mark out the circle on the ground. Charge the loop with an intention for developing a spiritual space by slowly walking clockwise around it from the inside. As you stroll, "draw" the circle once again by pointing with your index finger, envisioning the energetic connection in between your body and the circle's edge, keep in mind, you are developing a place of higher, more powerful energy than will exist on the outside of the circle. This is an act that requires learning and consistent practice. It is not strictly necessary. However, it is a time-honored part of the Wiccan tradition that numerous discover to be important.

Light the white and black candles and invite the God and Goddess (or the balanced forces of male and woman) to be present with you in the celebration. If you wish, call the quarters by turning to stand in each primary instructions, starting with North and moving clockwise. Verbally acknowledge each direction by name and its associated aspect, and request its energy to come into your circle. You are already incorporating signs of the Elements with the pentacle (Earth), the incense or oil (Air), the candles (Fire), and the cup (Water) so you might hold each of these items as you welcome the Elements, either instead of calling the quarters or as part of it.

Show on the abundance you've experienced in the past season. Identify seven things you are grateful for and state them aloud. These can be little things or bigger ones-- whatever you feel genuinely thankful for at this time. Ask for any aid you need with developing balance, keeping security, and letting go of something.

If you're using a spell candlelight, rub a drop or 2 of essential oil into it, or simply hold it in your hands for a couple of moments. Visualize yourself feeling safe and grateful for the abundance in your life, in excellent physical health, and emotionally balanced. Out loud, state this vision in whatever method appears most natural to you. You may just say, "I have whatever I require. I am in health. My life is balanced." Light the green candle as you say the words. Then "seal" the deal with the last expression. Many Witches use the following: "So let it be," "So mote it be," "Blessed Be," or "It is done." Whatever you select, make sure to knowingly launch your objectives into the higher worlds where they can be changed and manifest. Enjoy the flame for a few moments, feeling the favorable energies raised within you and all around you in the sacred area.

When you're ready, thank the Elements, then the Goddess and God for their existence. Close the circle by strolling around it counter-clockwise, releasing its energy into the Universe. (Note: Don't leave any candles ignored, but do let the spell candle stress out on its own, if at all possible.).

Over the next couple of weeks, continue the practice of recognizing abundance and revealing thankfulness. You might likewise observe any seeming imbalances in your life or wellness and choose to do what you can to remedy them. If you do so, you will see that deep space will support you!

What Does Manifestation Look Like?

When Witches speak of "symptom" or "success" concerning prayer, intention, or spellwork, what do they imply? You do not tend to hear fairytale-like stories about vast, overnight gains in one's lifestyle the day after working a spell, though anything can take place if all the best situations remain in place. What innovative professionals of the Craft understand is that practice is needed in the form of research study, time, and experiment. One likewise has to cultivate a mindset that is open to manifestation, to success, and positive and wonderful incidents.

This can be a hard routine to obtain and hold onto, and everybody has their blind spots now and once again, however with active practice, the wonders of deep space begin to unfold more progressively.

Let me show you how.

When upon a time, a young, aiming Witch met an older, far more skilled Witch at a folk festival, where they were both outdoor camping in the woods. As the celebration wound down and everyone was evacuating to leave, the two Witches decided to exchange their contact info. Neither had a writing implement, nor could they discover any in their tents or packs. Then suddenly, the more youthful Witch spotted a pencil, "randomly" resting on the forest flooring in between 2 trees. "Wow," said the older Witch. "Talk about manifesting!".

The more youthful Witch was confused. How was this an example of "manifesting"? The pencil hadn't fallen from the sky, or perhaps been suddenly provided by a passerby out of the blue. Sure, it was a welcome coincidence, however clearly some other individual had simply lost a pencil in that spot in the woods, and over a celebration weekend, those woods saw their fair share of human artifacts. Besides, no spell or necromancy had been performed. So how did this pencil count as a symptom?

The more youthful Witch was too accustomed to analyzing the possible causes of occasions to appreciate the synchronicity and Divine timing of this pencil's development into her reality. Instead of focusing on the inherent magic of this small event, she instinctively transferred to dismiss it in favor of the regular "logical" thinking instilled in her through cultural conditioning.

This is a difficulty faced by numerous who are brand-new to the Craft, however, with consistent determination to be available to the subtleties of truth below our "reasonable" experience, it ends up being much easier to recognize all type of manifestations, from the "little things" to much larger improvements in our lives.

There are a few essential components in this specific event that satisfy the conceptual requirements of symptoms. The pencil appeared in the ideal location at the best time. Second, it fulfilled a particular need that, if met, would be useful to both individuals included, and would harm no one. Third, it happened in such a way that was unforeseen, instead of as an outcome of searching in all the apparent, rational locations for something to compose with. Symptom typically comes in methods we might never have thought of or prepared for, and as an extra-nice touch, it took place in a natural setting: a forest of old, splendid trees.

Only as significantly, the pencil was acknowledged as a symptom by the older Witch, who understood from practice how to recognize and value it as such. She also realized that symptoms could happen with or without designated spellwork. Often deep space merely assists in minutes of requirement or crisis-- these occasions are sometimes called "wonders." Since the older Witch was well-grounded in magical principles, she was frequently able to plan for things right away and did so regularly, always growing in her capability to connect her power with the Divine.

Beyond routine, intention-setting, and spellwork, the practice of taking notes and acknowledging with appreciation is just as crucial to affective symptoms. As you start seeing synchronicities in your life, nevertheless small, take note and remember them. You may wish to tape incidents that appear considerable in a journal or Book of Shadows. You will discover that the more you take note of them, the more you will draw in positive symptoms in your life.

- **Keeping a Book of Shadows.**

The term "Book of Shadows" comes out of the Gardnerian Tradition, however, has been widely embraced and adjusted by eclectics, covens, and solitaries ever considering that. Keeping one is an excellent way for skilled and brand-new Witches alike to deepen their practice of the Craft.

You can consider your Book of Shadows as a sort of journal, particularly for wonderful and/or spiritual pursuits. The contents of a Book of Shadows are individual and will differ from Witch to Witch. Some keep detailed directions for rituals and spells, either borrowed from other sources or of their own innovation. Some diligently record the results of their magical workings, information about their individual deity alignments, or lists of specific herbs and stones they feel an affinity with. Others might free-write about their intentions for a certain routine or a brand-new season. This can likewise be a good location to tape-record relevant dreams or other signs and messages that enter into your life. It's often illuminating to revisit these at a later date and see underlying connections between apparently unassociated phenomena!

These are just a couple of tips for digging deeper into the world of Wicca and Witchcraft. As we've seen, it's a highly varied and broad faith with many possible opportunities to follow. No matter what you do, always follow your instinct when it comes to how, when, and if you want to start the course of the Craft.

CONCLUSION

Unlike the majority of other Western faiths, Wicca is extremely decentralized, there is no official sacred text, no main governing body, and this means there is nobody way to practice the religion.

With this in mind, it is extremely tough to create a novice's guide on this topic, simply because different Wiccans will interpret the various facets of the belive in a different way.

In this guide, I have actually attempted to provide an impartial technique, though unquestionably, my own experiences as a practicing Wiccan may have influenced certain areas of this book. Generally speaking, I have actually tried to cover the most "popular" technique in each chapter above, as this will make the information much easier to absorb, and you are likewise most likely to meet Wiccans with the very same set of beliefs that truly resonate with you.

There is no right or wrong. As long as you keep the Wiccan principles at heart, and never ever intentionally seek to damage others, you can practice Wicca in any way you see fit. I would actively encourage you to look for your own path. One of the very best things about Wicca is that your beliefs, interpretations, and views are extremely versatile. When you are just starting out, you are encouraged to check out and discover as much as possible, and so your initial beliefs are bound to be shaped by the guides you check out.

Over time, when you begin to embrace Wicca in your day-to-day life, you might have special surprises that re-shape your method of practicing this faith. What you think on day one might be extremely different from your beliefs on day 100, which could be a world apart from your views on day 1,000. It can be a lifelong journey, and even after years, you will still discover yourself finding out new things.

Remember: nobody can inform you how to practice Wicca, and the religion can indicate anything you want it to suggest to you. While I have provided the info in this guide as "appropriate," I remain in no chance implying that it is the only way to practice Wicca. If you check out other guides, there might be clashing details. And when you checked out another guide to the subject, you will likely encounter much more contrasting info!

I will leave you with that thought, as it is now time for you to begin your journey, and interpret the info presented to you in your way. I sincerely hoped you delighted in finding out about Wicca with me, as it is a subject close to my heart. It would suggest a good deal to me if you continue on your path towards Wicca, however, if you choose not to, I hope I have educated you on the belief system of the terrific people who pick to practice Wicca.